Walking the Trail of Death

Walking the Trail of Death
By Keith Drury
Marion, Indiana 2007
ISBN 978-0-359-94876-5

Copyright © 2007 by Keith Drury
Published by Keith Drury.
Second edition
Marion, Indiana   2007
Printed in the United States of America

Dedication

To Shirley Willard
Angel of the Trail of Death

Shirley Willard, Trail Angel

Acknowledgements

I owe a great debt to Shirley Willard for her service. Shirley had never met me when I walked into her town in northern Indiana the first week of May, 2006 as I began this journey. She adopted me like she had long before adopted the Trail of Death. She became my constant invisible angel working in the background. Dozens of times people showed up to help me along the journey because Shirley had been off-stage prompting them. She badgered newspaper editors until they finally relented, got into their cars and came out to write a story. She wanted this story to be told and retold. Her passionate enthusiasm for reminding America of the Trail of Death is indomitable. It was her persistence that brought into existence stone markers all across the entire route—more than one per day on their 60+ day route.

Frankly, when I completed this walk I had little desire to polish this manuscript to publish—even a short first run. I was weary of the story and wanted to forget the injustice and "move on." I had lived with the burden for two months and wanted to lay it aside. Besides, I had another book contract in my pocket so this story stayed in limbo. One editor said, "Nobody wants to hear about bad things we did in the past—just forget it." But Shirley badgered me and so here is *Walking the Trail of Death*, largely a result of Shirley's persistence. Beyond prodding me to finish, she offered her considerable skills as an historian and editor to improve the first edition of the book. But I caution the reader—this book has not been through a dozen drafts and edits. It is essentially "Blog-syle" writing or perhaps a traveler's journal written on the road. Most of it appeared on an actual blog that I posted as I walked.

There are others to thank as well. My daughter-in-law, Kathy Drury contacted television stations like Shirley had contacted newspaper editors. There were scores of folk along the way who showed kindness to me on this journey far above what could be imagined. They offered meals, snacks, friendship, company and sometimes people I had never met me offered guest rooms in their homes. I promise to all of you that I will "pay it forward" and I shall mention the names of these "trail angels" on the day's entry of my own story where you offered your kindness.

And I must express my love and appreciation to my wife, Sharon, who supported me in this walk. Her daily text messages, regular love letters sent to every post office stop along the way, and care packages of candy were a constant encouragement. Most of I give Sharon credit for squeezing time into her busy schedule as a Dean to visit me. Weekend after weekend she arranged to drive out and meet me for a day off. While every step I took was one step away from home, it was one step closer to the prearranged town ahead of me where I would meet you waiting for me so many weekends that kept me going.

Someone said to Socrates
that a certain man had grown no better by his travels.
"I should think not," he said:
"he took himself along with him."
                Michael de Montaigne

I am a better person
because of others I met on this way
for I am a poor walking companion for myself.

Foreword

I am neither an Indian nor an historian. I am a white man who is a minister and professor. I had lived in Indiana for decades and had never heard of the Trail of Death. A short article appeared in my local newspaper calling the Trail of Death, "Indiana's own Trail of Tears." Like most folk, I had heard the story of the forced removal of the Cherokee from the North Carolina area but I was ignorant of the many other removals going on all across America at the time. It was our government's national policy. I discovered Indiana had its own stories of tribes of Indians being removed from Indiana (ironically, "land of the Indians").

I got fascinated so much that I began to search for information on the forced relocation of Indiana's Potawatomi Indians to Kansas. I searched for primary sources—records from the actual time. When I found these I was ecstatic and began to devour each one on weekends, piecing together the unfolding story. Eventually I based my walk (and this book) on the following sources:

Two Sources

- **THE GOVERNMENT:** We still have the official journal of the government leader of this expedition (William Polke) though it was hand-written by his scribe. We also have several dozen letters sent by Polke to various officials. Also extant are letters from General/Senator Tipton who led the expedition to the Illinois state line and we have various other official letters from the Indian agent, Abel Pepper. There is also the "continuation journal" of Polke which records what happened to Polke after the Indians were dropped off in Kansas.

- **THE PRIEST**: As a minister, my greatest interest was a pastor's journey with his people. I found two sources: We still have this pastor's journal recording baptisms and funerals, along with sketchy references to the day's events. We also have Father Petit's vivid descriptions of events in letters to his family at home in France and to his Bishop in Vincennes, Indiana. I have coordinated the sketchy references in the journal with the longer descriptions in the latter and recorded the events of Petit on the day they happened, or sometimes the closest day that fits.

While reading these original sources I became so engrossed that I asked,

"What would it feel like to walk 660 miles from Indiana to Kansas?" The notion caught my imagination so powerfully I soon began planning to actually do it—walk the Trail of Death. I took along copies of all the primary sources so I could ponder the entries in each case on the actual day's walk where they had occurred. My goal was to bring together all the various sources into one day's entry adding my own experience 168 years after the original journey. I gathered old maps and new ones so I could trace their journey at each night's campsite. A special feature for me was the "pondering" I intended to do while walking—considering current issues like immigration, Indian mascots for sports teams, injustice, restitution and penance while walking.

So, here in this book I have brought together each of the primary sources in the daily entries producing four parts for each day:
- *That day's events* based on the official journal and various letters.
- *Father Petit's activities* for the day.
- *My own experiences* walking the trail following their path.
- *Pondering* larger questions of philosophy, theology or politics.

I use "Indians" here even though we have moved beyond that nomenclature. It was the term used in all of my sources but I di not prefer it.

This is not a fancy book. I don't expect many to read it. It essentially collects together my on-the-trail blogging day by day. The manuscript has been edited a bit since appearing on the Internet, but it is still a rough manuscript and should be read in an over-the-shoulder style—as if you have uncovered my raw diary and not a finished work. Since I expect a small readership I have not chosen to go the normal editing-publishing route of my other books. Rather this work will be available in the new emerging print-on-demand market.

I hope you find some benefit from my effort. This trip was difficult for many reasons, not the least of which was a continuing sense of guilt and shame for the whole sordid affair. However I am a better person for it in spite of traveling so much with myself. Others contributed deeply to my life on this journey; some have been dead for almost 170 years. I hope you will be angered by the *injustice* of these events, but more than that, I hope you will be inspired by the *courage and faith* of these people

--Keith Drury April 2, 2007

Day 0 --Mile 0
August 31-Sept. 3, 1838

The Potawatomi Indians who were living at Twin Lakes, Indiana were a peaceful band so they willingly attended a unity conference with whites when invited. The conference was a trick. While gathered under this pretense they were surrounded by General Tipton with a hundred of the Indiana volunteer militia who fired off their guns and took the Indians prisoners beginning their forced "removal" to Kansas.

Two years earlier the Potawatomi had "sold" their land to the government by treaty. They were to be transported west to a great promised land in Kansas where they understood there would be houses and cultivated fields awaiting them. Most Chiefs (having been served generous amounts of free alcohol) had signed the treaties and sold their land. Much of this income was already gone—paid to traders who had been selling them expensive goods and food on credit. The Indians signed the treaty, the government first paid off the traders' debts, and then if there was any left, the Indians got it. There was seldom any left. The irony is they had sold their land and remained poor. After the treaties were signed and ratified, the Potawatomi had two years to vacate. The two years were up. General Tipton intended to get rid of "the Indian Problem" forever.

Chief Menominee would not sign or sell. This "Potawatomi preacher" taught and practiced abstinence from alcohol and practiced what he preached—he never lost control of his senses enough to make his mark on the treaty sacrificing his land to the government (usually at the rate of about $1 an acre). Menomonee insisted he'd just stay where he was—in the state of Indiana, the "land of the Indians."

It made no difference. The Indians who had already sold their land, along with Menominee who hadn't, were rounded up like cattle and forced to "emigrate" west across the Mississippi River where they would be out of the way. This was supposed to be the final solution to "the Indian problem." Menominee along with other chiefs were put in a jail wagon as they rounded up other stragglers for the journey west. The Indians' houses and log cabins in their village were burned and the tribe was forced to pack up and begin moving west. All this happened in less than a week—men, women, children, babies and grandparents—the whole village was forced at gunpoint to march west.

General Tipton, a U.S. Senator from Indiana, would lead the southward journey to the Wabash River and from there westerly to Kansas—almost a thousand Potawatomi were captured and forced west in this "emigration ."

Menominee's followers were devout Catholics. In this story the *Indians* are the real believers and their escorts act far below a Christian standard. The tribe even had a priest—Father Benjamin Petit who had been serving them faithfully and he wanted to accompany them on this painful journey.

FATHER PETIT was not present when the Potawatomi were captured. He had been working against the forced emigration which he knew was looming. But he had to be careful—he was not a US Citizen, but a French missionary—and the US government was inclined to expel "foreigners" who "stirred up the Indians." Petit's predecessor had been pressured to leave before he died for just such causes. A priest had to walk a fine line between representing his congregation's best interests and appearing to be a foreign troublemaker. Petit had been busy. He had just performed 14 baptisms, two marriages and taking numerous confessions along with visiting many sick before he returned to South Bend, which was his base of operations for his itinerant missionary enterprise to the Potawatomi Indians. He reported in his diary: *"I am a little tired out—the emigration agents harass, accuse, flatter me; threaten the Indians."* He feared armed bloodshed most of all. He had assured the troops his Indians would not resist with arms. But he had not left his Indian-built log chapel at Twin Lakes willingly. On August 5th about a month before the militia showed up, the government took possession of his log church the devoted Catholic Indians had so lovingly constructed. And he lost his house. As the interior of the church was stripped, Petit cried along with the sobbing of his devout Christian congregation who stood by. Petit bid farewell to his Indian congregation and left the village in tears. He returned to his South Bend headquarters—on the land that would eventually become Notre Dame University.

AS FOR ME, I intend to follow the Indian's route west the 660 miles to Kansas from Twin Lakes, Indiana, near Plymouth, Indiana. I have the first half of the summer—May and June of 2006. I am Keith Drury, an Associate Professor of Religion at Indiana Wesleyan University. A copy of the official journal of the militia describing each day and their campsites along the way will guide me along with the letters and personal journal of Father Petit the priest. I also have copies of letters sent from the two men who led the forced emigration —Senator/General John Tipton who started out leading the group and letters from Judge William Polke who took over once the party left Indiana. These primary sources serve as my guidebook—both to the route and campsites along the way. I will try to relive what these Indians experienced almost 170 year ago. Mostly I want to ponder the injustice of it all day by day for the next two months—the same amount of time it took the original Indians to complete the journey in 1838. I may not always be able to camp in the exact spot as the Indians did (sometimes it will be in the middle of a housing development). And sometimes I may walk a bit off their path, but my research on roads and routes of these states in 1838 will enable me to walk fairly close to their original route. I won't be walking "paths" and neither did they. There were roads all the way to Kansas City at the time—only after they passed into Kansas the "trace" sometimes disappears.

I'VE BEEN THINKING about Menominee. There were more than a dozen chiefs involved with this Indian removal, yet Menominee is the one remembered most. Is he admired because he did what we all think every chief should have done—refuse to sell? The other chiefs got money. Menominee got nothing. Or, perhaps what he got lasted much longer than money.

Statue of Menominee at Twin lakes, Indiana -- Day 0

Day 1 Chippeway, Indiana --Mile 21
Sept 4, 1838

The first day of a long journey often yields longer miles than later days. You'd think the opposite would be true—that the early days of a trek would yield lower miles so that when the walker "got into shape" they'd increase their miles. But actually during the first day one's spirit is high, drudgery has not yet set in, and there are no blisters or muscle cramps to slow one down, so, often the first burst of walking gets the walker more miles.

This was only half true for the Potawatomi Indians. Yes, they did walk 21 miles their first day out—longer than any other single day for the next six weeks. But high spirit was not the reason. Water was.

The summer of 1838 brought a severe drought to the "Northwest USA" (as Indiana was considered to be at the time). The creeks were dry, streams offered only stagnant pools of water and the "emigrating party" was forced to plan their journey so they could camp near water sources. This meant some days they stopped sooner than they wanted to, and other days they had to walk further—as on this day, Tuesday September 4, 1838, when they walked 21 miles.

The official journal describes the day thus: *"The day was exceedingly sultry, and the roads choked with dust."* No wonder. 958 Indians with their 285 horses plus a hundred militia who were "escorting" these Indians west traveled the dusty "Michigan Road" south toward "Chippeway " (a few miles north of present day Rochester, Indiana) where they spent their first night. This town no longer exists but was on the Michigan Road where it crossed the Tippecanoe River two miles north of Rochester, Indiana. As was their custom, the Indians traveled in single file making a line three miles long, according to a newspaper account (Delphi, Indiana). Such a single file line would raise up from the dry road a billowing cloud of dust which would become unbearable for those in the back of the line. Hot and thirsty with dust in their ears, eyes, and mouths, the Indians trudged on day after day. The scarcity of water would plague them for the next four weeks. And so would death.

FATHER PETIT was not with the group at this time. He was in South Bend. He had worked faithfully to fight the impending injustice, including even arranging for the chiefs to travel to Washington D.C. for a meeting with Andrew Jackson, the US President. Alas, nothing worked. The country had made up its mind about solving "the Indian problem" and it was too late to talk. Forced removal to the west became inevitable. Petit's backup plan was to accompany his beloved congregation on their westward journey—to minister to them and to intervene for them on the way. Petit was after all, a priest not a politician.

Petit's Bishop refused to let him go. Bishop Brute of Vincennes, Indiana wisely wanted to avoid the appearance of collaboration with the government in this nasty enterprise. He would not give Petit permission to accompany his Indians. Father Petit became sick for the next three weeks with "the fever." We do not know what this fever was but it could have been typhoid fever or even Cholera. Whatever, Petit came down with this fever repeatedly over the next three months. This current bout lasted three weeks. But even while suffering the fever, his journal shows he went to visit the sick at Pokagon's tribe of Potawatomi. And certainly he thought continually about the Twin Lakes Indians and their impending fate—he had heard nothing from them for almost a month.

AS FOR ME, scarcity of water is not my problem—but an abundance of it. I started this walk in pouring rain and it has continued all day long with only one break for me on the porch of an empty Child Evangelism Fellowship office where I ate the whole 8 oz. package of "Swedish fish" sent to me by Josh Jackson—my only food for the day. Back on the road after my candy-lunch I sloshed on until I lay down for the night soaked and exhausted several miles short of the Potawatomi camp at Argos, Indiana. I found a partially finished new house where I found shelter from the pouring rains—the roof was finished but no doors installed yet. I rolled out my sleeping bag in the back "bedroom" chuckling that the people living here later would never know they entertained their first house guest before they moved in. It rained all night with cracking thunder and I awakened frequently but totaled 13 hours of sleep by the time it was light

Why am I doing this walk? At first glance it seems like *guilt*, but that's not really it. My great-great Grandparents were digging in the coalmines in England at this time—so I carry no family blame for this injustice. Perhaps *shame* is a better word. In some ways I'm ashamed of what my race and my nation did to the Indians. But that's not exactly the right word either. As I began to walk this morning at the statue of Menominee the word that emerges strongest may be *mourning*. I have a sense of sadness and pain for what the Potawatomi Indians experienced and I want to identify with it. The Bible says, "Blessed are those who mourn." I am exploring the blessedness of this mourning on this trek. I'm setting aside two months to mourn with the Potawatomi and I think I can do that best by actually retracing their route step by step. Then again what do I know? How do I know on the first day why I'm doing this? Maybe the reasons will change as I go along.

I'VE BEEN THINKING about religion. Before the white man arrived, the Potawatomi already believed in God. Who was that god? They had no Bible, and had never heard of Jesus Christ. But Abraham, Isaac and Jacob had no Bible and had never heard of Jesus Christ. Was the *Great Spirit* to whom the Native Americans prayed the same god to whom Abraham prayed? I'm wondering about that tonight as I fall asleep.

The Michigan Road connecting the Ohio River with Michigan was built on Potawatomi land that had been purchased by an earlier treaty.

Day 2 --Mud Creek, Indiana --Mile 30
Sept 5, 1838

I walked quickly the next morning to Chippeway, on the Tippecanoe River the site of the Potawatomi's first campsite of the journey. If it had not been raining so hard yesterday I would have walked to here. I am already playing catch-up to their pace. On their very first night here on the river twenty Indians escaped. Despite a band of militia sent to round them up, they were never found. Who knows, maybe they faded into the population and thousands of people in Indiana are now their progeny? The Indians' trip today was a short one–nine miles to Mud Creek which was aptly named then, or at least it is descriptive of the creek today. At this campsite the first death occurred on this "Trail of Death." The death would be the first fruit of many more to come, mostly children and the elderly. One can imagine the sorrow around one of those late-night cooking fires where the mourning family prepared their daily rations of beef and flour. A mother's child had died. Yet around another cooking fire there was joy—a child was also born this second night. Such is life—a blending of sorrow and joy, sickness and health, evil and good.

FATHER PETIT was still sick with the fever and by this day had gone to Bertrand, Michigan to recuperate. Today he heard the news: *"the Indians are prisoners of war"* as he wrote it in his journal. He received word from General Tipton requesting him to join the forced emigration. He sent back his answer refusing, explaining that his Bishop would not allow it. How this must have hurt Petit. The right place for a true shepherd is among his sheep—especially when they are hurting. Yet a pastor (or at least a Catholic Priest) must also submit to church authority. Petit obeyed his Bishop with his body, but his mind certainly must have been yearning to be with his faithful Christian congregation. The pain of loving *in absentia* may have hurt more than his fever. Then on this day Petit's Bishop showed up suddenly. The Bishop announced they together would head to Logansport. Full of hope that the Bishop might change his mind, Petit must have jumped at the chance to travel southward toward his congregation on this day. He wrote in a letter to his family that on this morning the Bishop on his return from Chicago walked into Petit's room announcing *"My son, in an hour we depart for Logansport."* Petit needed no more words to get ready.

AS FOR ME I sloshed on today largely depressed at the rain. Just as I grumbled to myself wondering "Why did I decide to do this?" a car stopped across the road and a head stuck out the window asking, "You still walkin'? It was Bill Willard who quickly arranged for his wife Shirley to meet us for lunch as soon as I got the next few miles into the town of Rochester. Here this couple treated me to a huge lunch special at the Evergreen Café, which I topped off with home-made cherry pie and about 40 cups of coffee. At one point Shirley asked, 'Do you eat this much always when you walk?" Shirley Willard probably knows more about the Potawatomi Trail of Death than any person alive. She is a passionate historian of the route and a friend of the Potawatomi. She brought along her huge collection of maps of the Indiana route, which she is arranging to put online for others to access. Consulting her maps, I was able to correct my own maps all the way to the Illinois line. She promised to send me her information for the later states when I got there. Leaving the Evergreen café I was several pounds heavier but felt 20 pounds lighter after the warm conversation with these new friends. I soon passed Mud Creek mentioned above and walked to the edge of Fulton, Indiana, where I found an inviting cemetery at the edge of town in which I (probably illegally) spent my night sleeping between Clara and James, having to put up my tiny tarp because of gigantic thunderstorms which kept me awake most of the night.

I'VE BEEN THINKING TONIGHT about dead people. Who visits these graves? Does anyone beside homeless people like me ever visit Clara and James? Sure, for the first few decades relatives might come, but what about after that? Will people visit my grave? Why? And, I'm wondering why we put head stones with our names carved in them? Do we hope someone will care about us after we're gone and come looking for our name? I think Menominee was eventually buried in Kansas and I doubt if he has a carved headstone. Yet we remember him for what he *did* not for where his body was buried. I think that I also would rather be remembered for what I did while living than where I was placed after dying.

Day 3 to Logansport, Indiana --Mile 47
Sept 6, 1838

The "journal of the migrating party" has only a short paragraph for today, though the group walked 17 miles into Logansport and to the shore of the Wabash River. The only entry of note reported nine Indians who had been left sick at the first night's campsite (Chippeway) had caught up to the group today. Logansport was a major town and in some ways the official jumping off point for this journey west. It was Tipton's town (he was later buried here). At Logansport the Indians would turn west.

Also in Logansport they would leave the "Michigan Road" which was constructed just eight years before. It was Indiana's pride—a road connecting the Ohio River to Michigan–from Madison on the Ohio river north to Michigan City. It was built on Potawatomi land that had been purchased by an earlier treaty. On this land the government built the road and also sold adjacent parcels to white settlers which paid for the road's construction—a profitable business enterprise of sorts. It was during this decade—the 1830's—that Indiana also saw the National Road (or Cumberland Road—present US 40) enter Indiana to eventually cross the Michigan road at Indianapolis forming a giant plus sign on the state.

AS FOR ME the rain slowed today. I had a straightaway walk into town with no stores on the route except a quick cup of coffee and microwave sausage and egg sandwich at the Fulton, Indiana, gas station. Today a border collie took a liking to me. He seemed determined to follow me all the way to Kansas. Nothing I did could discourage him and make him go home. I scolded him, shouted at him, and even threw sticks and stones at him to persuade him to go home but he refused. He would look at me with his perplexed sad brown eyes as if to say, "I know you really want a partner for this trip—and even if you throw stones at me I will just follow a stone's throw away from you." What's a fella' to do? I looked for bigger stones. The dog was smart—he could judge my range. It became a kind of game for him I think—he would follow just a few feet beyond my range then watch my stones fall short with pity for me. I kept wondering if he was some child's pet back behind me. When he started walking right down the middle of route 25 playing chicken with the coming eighteen-wheelers as they screeched to a halt, I knew I had to do something before he got killed. I wondered why cars and trucks automatically slow down when there is a dog nearby but do not even hit their brakes for a person. I can tell the moment a truck driver spies the dog in the grass. They leave off their accelerator and start to coast. The "I brake for animals" bumper stickers must be working. But, apparently there are no "I brake for walkers" stickers. I guess they know I won't leap out in front of them like this suicidal dog does. After a pick-up truck slammed on his brakes so hard he fishtailed partially into the ditch to avoid hitting "my" dog I decided I had enough. I took him to the next house and asked the owner to tie him up for an hour then let him loose so he'd go home. This is how I lost my first walking companion on this trip. I chuckled at it as I walked away. I do not plan to treat any future human companions this way.

The rain lifted today but blisters arrived—on my right foot. The right foot is a target of pain for road walkers. We generally walk facing the traffic and the road is "crowned" meaning my right foot feels about a quarter inch "longer" than my left foot which throws everything off balance and causes considerable more pounding to happen in the right foot over the left. I took two long breaks today to dry out my feet, hoping the blisters would leave. They didn't. It was with these blisters that I limped the final 5 miles into Logansport.

In Logansport I found a real treat that lifted my spirits above blisters. Brook, a recent graduate of Indiana Wesleyan University is the pastor of a church directly on the route right beside the Eel River before it flows into the Wabash. Actually he lives about 100 yards or so from the actual site of the Potawatomi campsite. Brook and I went out for a steak dinner at Ponderosa to celebrate my not quitting yet. We both returned to the all-you-can-eat buffet at least 17 times though I had a better excuse to do so than him. Brook's wife Jill is a nurse. We drove to the Post Office where I collected my mail, leaving a forwarding notice for any mail coming after I leave. I'm ahead of "schedule" so far, but my blisters will shave off that margin soon enough. After sleeping next to Clara and James in the Fulton cemetery the night before, I now get to sleep on a real bed with myself. Ah, such luxury! I'm falling asleep almost forgetting the burning blisters on my feet. The Potawatomi spent four nights here in Logansport—but that's another story, for now I am going to bed in a *bed*.

I'VE BEEN THINKING about how easy my walk is. The Potawatomi had no friendly homes to stop at, few village stores to shop in, and little good water to drink—often no water at all. My walk is a cakewalk compared to theirs. I'm no hero taking this walk. I'm just an ordinary guy trying to identify with the pain of another group 158 years ago. I know I'll never be able to fully understand that pain any more than a young pastor can understand the pain of an old woman who has just lost her husband. But he can try. So can I. So I will keep walking.

Day 4-6 in Logansport, Indiana --Mile 47
Sept. 7-9, 1838

Once the Potawatomi reached Logansport the Indians collapsed into sickness. It is strange how the third and fourth days of a journey can be the hardest of a trek. People quit their jobs every spring intent on hiking the entire Appalachian Trail and they start at Springer Mountain in Georgia. Yet three days later in Suches, Georgia, as many as 10% of these "thru-hikers" give up and go home. The euphoria of the first day wears off and they are hit with the drudgery of trail life. Three days is just long enough for blisters to develop and for most of the fun to have leaked away.

The Potawatomi weren't just suffering from blisters but were probably facing Typhoid. We don't know for sure but "the fever" or general sickness they experienced that year is likely to have been Typhoid, which they picked up from the stagnant water. Whatever, at Logansport a great many fell sick. The Indians stayed in town the entire weekend—camping Thursday night on the Eel River where it meets the Wabash and staying through Monday morning—a full weekend of sickness and death.

On Friday morning a child died, the second death of the journey. On Saturday a three-year-old child died and was buried. On Sunday physicians came into the camp to do a check-up and reported 300 cases of sickness. By Sunday a *"kind of medical hospital"* was erected and the doctors began treatments. Medical treatment wasn't much in those days: tea, sugar and rest. Probably the rest without the tea and sugar would have done as much good. On Sunday another child died during the day and still another after dark making five children dead in the first six days of this journey. The children are always the first to go. Long walking and disease takes the weakest and most vulnerable first—the kids.

Yet amidst all the sickness and death a great worship service was held on Sunday evening with Bishop Brute presiding (the Catholic Bishop from Vincennes and supervisor of Father Petit). Almost a thousand Indians attended. Frontier artist George Winter was an eyewitness and sketched the scene. Many of the Potawatomi were devout Catholic Christians. Even though Menominee had flirted for a while with Baptists, he and his tribe were Catholics at heart. The tribe had been evangelized by Jesuit missionaries originally years before but had not had a Catholic priest for 60 years, yet they had continued to faithfully hold morning and evening prayers *"after the fashion of the Catholics"* all those years. They held these prayer and preaching services (without the Eucharist) for decades with no missionary presence! No wonder when the "black robes" returned they became loyal and devout followers. No wonder they had no trouble turning out for the Sunday evening mass at Logansport even though a third of them were sick. Yes, we should remember there were Potawatomi who were Baptists on this trip too and others who continued traditional religious practices. I recognize this but as a Christian minister, I am especially interested in the story of the Catholic congregation and their pastor, Father Petit. If there were near a thousand Indians attending this mass I am wondering if the Baptists and those who practiced traditional religion attended the mass as well and just did not partake of the Eucharist?

FATHER PETIT presided at that service, having left South Bend on September 5 accompanying his Bishop to Logansport. On their arrival the Bishop had concealed Petit, perhaps not wanting to have the Indians clamor for their pastor or maybe he had not made up his mind to let Petit go on the trip yet. Petit may have seen another opportunity to get him to relent and so he begged again for permission to accompany the Indians west. He was refused again. He wrote in his journal, *"another refuses to permit me to accompany the emigration to the Mississippi—I will not ask again."* Petit gave up. He would have to let his Indians travel this lonely *via dolorosa* on their own without his pastoral services.

On the morning of the September 7 the Bishop suddenly changed his mind. I think it was observing the devotion of the Potawatomi at the afternoon service that moved him. Or maybe when he saw the desperate situation of 300 sick Indians he was moved—three hundred sick parishioners are enough to even move a Bishop's heart! Then again, it may have been the persuasive politician's arguments from Senator/General Tipton who might have seen Petit as a man who could keep the Indians quiet and under control while the whites executed this shameful deed. Perhaps it was a combination of several of these factors, though I prefer the softening of heart theory mostly because I want it to have happened that way. The political persuasion of a US senator may be more likely, I will admit. We do know that Petit entered this into his journal for the day, *"I receive permission—General Tipton's and Judge Polke's request,"* after which he goes on to describe the mass, vespers and confirmation at the camp. Maybe both Tipton and Polke together had persuaded the Bishop to permit Petit to accompany the Indians. Whatever, pastor Petit celebrated the mass Sunday evening knowing that he could follow his congregation to Kansas. When Petit shows up publicly his congregants gather to receive his blessing and the General remarked, *"This man has more power here than I."* It was true. Whenever religious leaders have more power than politicians and military leaders, they soon will face an attempt to destroy them or to seduce and use their power for political purposes. The Indians had little reason to trust any white man but they did trust Father Petit with an astonishing level. Petit would not let them down.

The Bishop was in Logansport to consecrate the Logansport church while Petit officiated at the camp service. Petit believe this "coincidence" was ordained by Providence. After dedicating the church Bishop Brute' returned to the camp to perform an afternoon confirmation of about 20 of Petit's newly baptized converts. The Bishop described the event in a report later telling how the vespers were sung in the Indian language. This is one evidence of the "missiology" of Petit who apparently refused to reject the native language and allowed for its use in worship. After the afternoon service Petit may have persuaded his Bishop to accompany him to the sick tents where they ministered. He described one receiving Extreme Unction or "Last rites" and another receiving baptism, then closed his letter describing the two people with the phrase, "*both died that night.*"

AS FOR ME I did not stay any extra days in Logansport. My feet argued for a few days off insisting that they had Typhoid too or something worse. My back chimed in suggesting that another night in a real bed would be a great tonic as well. But my head cast the deciding vote and I leaped forward from the Indian's day three to day seven in one day's walking.

I'VE BEEN THINKING about Petit's obedience. This kind of thinking is so alien to us today. When we think something is right, we "just do it." We would probably claim "God told me to go with the Indians" and we'd ignore our stilted religious superiors. If our religious superior commanded us to stay when we thought God wanted us to go, we'd call the leader corrupt and label ourselves a hero for ignoring them. Americans are always praising the person who can say, "I did it my way." Not Petit. He submitted to his Bishop, and eventually got what he wanted anyway. I admire him. However, submission does not always work out so neatly that we always get what we want anyway.

Day 7 Winnemac's old village, Indiana --Mile 57
Sept. 10, 1838

The Potawatomi left Logansport Monday morning. Since we know that tea and sugar are feeble remedies for typhoid, it must have been the rest that helped for they got off by 10 a.m. At this point the Indians turned west for the first time. They had first headed east several miles from Twin Lakes to pick up the Michigan Road, and then they walked south on that road to Logansport. Now they turned west along the Wabash River toward Kansas. It took the Potawatomi seven hours to cover the ten miles along the north shore of the Wabash River from Logansport to the former site of Chief Winnemac's village. The village was already a "former site." Twin Lakes (that the Potawatomi had left) had now joined this designation as a "former site" of a village.

The atmosphere of the journey might have shifted at this point. The route now lay along the Wabash River and most likely was more shaded then their walk along the Michigan road. The Wabash and Erie Canal was under construction at the time (having been already finished west to Logansport) so they may have walked along the developing towpath of this famous canal. If they did, the Potawatomi and the canal were related in other ways.

Indiana had also purchased from the Potawatomi the land for the Wabash and Erie Canal. The scheme was clever: Buy the land cheap from the Indians, sell it at a couple hundred percent markups to white settlers, and use the profits to build canals like the Erie and Wabash Canal here.

The Wabash and Erie Canal was the longest canal in the USA, connecting Lake Erie and the eastern states with the Mississippi River via the Wabash River. Begun in Ft. Wayne, the highest point on the route (hence the city's nickname "Summit City"), the canal originally was intended only to get to the Wabash River which was purported to be deep enough to let boats travel all the way to New Orleans. Alas, someone didn't do their homework—the Wabash River was too shallow for the heavily laden canal boats and the canal eventually had to be continued all the way to Evansville to make the connection with the Ohio River. In the process the scheme bankrupted the state government, which was unable to even pay back the interest on the bonds issued. This collapse influenced the state to write a new constitution in 1851. The new constitution changed forever how Indiana could borrow money. Canals were the Great Big Idea of the day. Owners had made millions on canals in Pennsylvania and New York. Once a canal was established the price of shipping dropped by ten times—this would be like gasoline dropping from $3 gallon to 30 cents just by getting the state to build a canal to your town. Most everyone in those days thus became a canal booster. It did not work out so well for Indiana. Indiana's canals came too late. The railroad was already invented when the first section of Indiana's canal was dedicated. Railroads got stuff to towns just as cheap and far faster. Railroads did in the canals; just like today trucking and air travel seems to be returning the favor to the railroads.

I wonder how the Potawatomi saw a great public works project like this canal. Did they see it as a prime example of the white man's supposed supremacy? Crews of the latest immigrants (including especially Irish laborers) were busily digging and building up the sides of the canal. Surveyors were carefully measuring the fall of land to make sure the flow would be right. Masons were building great stone locks. It must have appeared to the Potawatomi an impressive achievement of the white man. All these "tribes" of white men were banding together to build their own river. If they were impressed they would have only needed to come back in a few years to be less impressed. In less than one generation this canal fell into disrepair and people walking it today must have a trained eye to even spy the indentation where it once sliced across the state as "The Answer" to the state's economic challenges. It is easier to find a Potawatomi in these parts today than the site of the Wabash and Erie Canal.

The Potawatomi made camp at Winnemac's old site. A man died today while they were traveling. He had been sick since Logansport. He was the first adult to die on the trek. After coming into camp another child died.

FATHER PETIT was headed north on this day. As the Indians left headed westward down the Wabash River, Father Petit was headed north to South Bend to collect the gear he would need for a multi-month journey ahead of him. He hoped to gather his baggage and quickly catch the Indians. It will take longer than he hoped. I think he may have regretted doubling back to gather his gear before long. People always think they need more stuff on a journey than they need. On this day Petit traveled part way back to South Bend before he slept—he was headed away from his flock.

AS FOR ME, my former student Pastor Brook fixed a gigantic breakfast of eggs, bacon, and pancakes complete with home-boiled-down maple syrup before I headed west. I am enjoying the shaded "Towpath Road" along the beautiful Wabash River. What a change from the last few days where I was constantly turning around to pick up my hat blown off by eighteen wheelers (purposely?) driving a bit too close to me. Here on this forgotten road I see only one or two cars per hour. I am walking amidst trillium, wild phlox, blue and white violets, and asters. Everywhere flowers are blooming and in the fields the corn is about a half inch high. My blisters are painful I am taking a full shoes-off rest stop every 3-4 miles but the day is bright and the sun is beautiful. By early afternoon I reached Winnemac's village site and took a leisurely break before walking on a few miles to a delightful ridge. I scrambled up the ridge where I found a view of the rich bottomland and river and pitched my tarp for the night. I ate half of Josh Jackson's care package I received at the Logansport Post Office for lunch, and for dinner I ate the rest. For dessert I had a packet of Reece's Pieces sent to me by Sharon. I am rich!

I fell asleep long before dark and only awakened a few times through the night. Once, the raindrops on the tarp woke me up, and twice howling coyotes awakened me. Two other times deer awoke me as they passed my tarp on their way to the Wabash. I checked in on my cell phone messages from the ridge tonight and I have no messages from hiking partners who might want to join me the coming week. However, I had messages from three people interested in joining me the following week—Kevin Wright, a student at Duke Divinity school; Phil Woodbury, a physician from Indianapolis; and Jason Denniston, a pastor from Indiana. My cell phone service goes in and out along the Wabash, so we'll see who (if any) of these three actually shows up. All of us tend to think a journey like this is a great idea until the day we actually are supposed to leave on it. So I'm used to people planning to hike with me, and then backing out at the last minute.

I'VE BEEN THINKING tonight about *revelation*. Theologically the term *revelation* has to do with God revealing Himself to humans. Some of the classic avenues of revelation include God revealing Himself to humans through the Bible, in Jesus Christ, in nature and sometimes directly to the person as in a dream or vision. The white man brought to America the Bible and the gospel of Jesus Christ, but the Indians had the other two channels before the white man arrived. What *revelation* of God did the Indians get from nature? Did God appear directly to some Indians like God appeared to Jacob in a dream? Jacob had no Bible nor Ten Commandments, or had ever heard of Jesus Christ. Did the Potawatomi have their own editions of Melchesidek? What would I believe about God if I only had natural revelation? If I had been born in America in 1300, how would God have revealed Himself? What would I have had to do to be "saved"?

Day 8 Pleasant Run, Indiana –Mile 74
Sept. 11, 1838

The trip to Pleasant Run was one of the happiest entries in the official journal. The route led over open, Champaign country *"which circumstance rendered the traveling more pleasant than that of any previous day."* The sick among the Indians seemed to *"be recruiting"* and the writer of the journal hopefully reported, *"everything bids fair for a comfortable and prosperous emigration."*

The journal-keeper went on to say (Jesse Douglas was the scribe) *"If we may be allowed to judge from the gayety of our encampments—the bright smiles that gild the sunny faces of our unhappy wards, and the contentment which seems to mark the sufferance of imposed restrictions, we may safely calculate upon the pleasantest and happiest emigration west."*

Who knows what the truth was? Pleasantness can be in the eyes of the beholder. Certainly it was not pleasant to Chief Menominee. He was forced to travel in a jail wagon bouncing along caged up for no other crime than his refusal to sell land rightfully belonging to him that had been granted by treaty with the US government. Certainly it was not a happy occasion for the parents of the many children who had already died along the route. Nevertheless camp was made at Pleasant Run, north of Pittsburg, Indiana, and seventeen miles south of Winnemac's old village. Pleasant Run is indeed a pleasant place today—a delightful shady creek that almost seems to emanate invisible invitations that all backpackers understand: "Here's a great place to camp." Whether the writer of the journal reflects the majority of the Indians' feeling we do not know. At least on this day there was one bit of good news: nobody died.

FATHER PETIT arrived in South Bend today about noon, knowing that each day he traveled north his precious congregation was headed south and west multiplying the distance between them. Petit must have been in a rush. I think he might have already regretted his return for his baggage. Who knows? Immediately he started packing but pastoral duties interrupted him. They always do. And old sick woman (the mother of Black Wolf) sought to give her confession. She had been present when General Tipton's militia had discharged their muskets to terrify and intimidate the Indians. She was so frightened she ran and hid herself in the woods where she stayed the next six days without food. Finally she had found a dead pheasant and ate that. But she was unable to walk due to a severe wound in her foot. After six days of hiding and hunger, another Indian had come upon her, put her on his horse and taken her to a Frenchman's house near South Bend. Father Petit, who had returned to pack, arrived and was then called to the house to hear her confession. He would care for this pastoral duty in spite of his desire to get moving west. But there were other people in need as well. There was a French woman, (Mademoiselle Campeau) who was dying, along with Madame Belley so he delayed his departure even more to minister to these folk and their families. Every moment he delayed meant the "emigration" added more miles between them. He must have squeezed in his packing between these pastoral duties and dropped into bed relieved that on the morning he would head south again so at least he would be headed the same direction as his parishioners.

AS FOR ME I walked past Pleasant Run. In fact this is why I have a bit of doubt about the journal writer's positive point of view. He recorded 17 miles for the day and I whizzed through it in a half day while shuffling slowly. I've done that—optimistically guessed my mileage longer than it was when I was particularly feeling good about the pathway and myself. But I really can't argue with him. He was using dead reckoning and so am I, so until I re-travel this route with an automobile or bicycle I'll have to take his word for it and give myself 20 miles credit by mid-afternoon. (Those who've trekked with me in the past will doubt their numbers too, as will any long distance walker.) So far I'd say the journal has been right on the money in listing miles.

I walked all day in the bright sunshine without my hat until my skin started to tingle. Why does sunburn feel so nice while you're getting it? Last night's meal of Gummy Bears and Reece's Pieces had worn off by noon so I stopped at a farmhouse and offered to buy a can of beans or can of whatever they'd offer for a dollar. The woman inside happily returned and said, "You can't buy it—it's yours" handing me a can of condensed vegetable soup. Down the street I opened the can and ate it cold. How good something tastes is directly related to how hungry a person is. I was hungry.

I walked into Pittsburg since I was now feeling just as optimistic as the journal writer. At US 421 I left the route and walked a mile or so into the town of Delphi, Indiana where I treated myself to a huge breakfast erasing the aftertaste of the too-condensed soup. I mailed some letters, then went to the Laundromat and quartered the dampness out of my sleeping bag. There I met Barbara Humphrey and we struck up a conversation about my journey. It turns out Barbara's grandfather was a full Potawatomi and she recited several stories that had been passed down in her family. Next I found the Delphi public library where the crew was especially helpful in letting me use a computer long after an ordinary person should have moved on.

During the evening I met Will and Marsha on the first gravel road I've walked so far. They showed me a morel mushroom the size of a person's hand and once they discovered the nature of my walk they drove home and came back at dusk with a full meal for me—hot ham and beans, macaroni salad, a couple of colas, a half pound of cheese, fresh bread and enough napkins for a Sunday school picnic. "We just wanted to help you on your way" they said then headed back home. Propped against a fence I feasted sumptuously, then found a secluded wood at the edge of a field and slept it off. Or tried to. Tonight was the first night I was joined by mosquitoes along with two sets of farmhouse dogs who barked the day's news back and forth to each other until about midnight when they apparently ran out of gossip. Finally the dogs and I went to sleep and let the mosquitoes do their work in silence. Thanks Will, and Marsha, for a wonderful dinner!

Just like the Potawatomi, today was for me my best day yet on this trek. Why? Was I influenced by their journal? Is it my anticipation of seeing Sharon tomorrow and the successful end of my first week's walking? Or was it the *spirit* of place? Do some places have a spirit of happiness and others sadness? Or is it all in my head—and theirs? The Indians believed some places bode ill or good will and passing through those spots affected the person. So do the modern Christian Charismatics. Are they right? Who knows? Maybe it is a combination of these things. But as I lay down tonight I felt better than any night yet. Curious.

I'VE BEEN THINKING about terrorism all day. I can't escape the picture of Black Wolf's mother hiding in terror for six days without food then eating a dead pheasant after Tipton's men discharged their muskets to terrify the Indians. Americans consider "terrorism" something an evil radical group carries out on a large peaceful people. We'd like to forget than the powerful and mighty can unleash terrorism as well. Tonight I go to sleep with mixed feelings—happiness from the wonderful day's "pleasant" walk and shame for the Senator from Indiana—John Tipton. I wonder if he felt any shame.

Day 9 -- Battleground, Indiana – Mile 89
Sept. 12, 1838

By 11 a.m. this day the Potawatomi forded the Tippecanoe River –the same river they had spent their first night camped along (at Chippeway) though at this point it is a much larger body of water. Within an hour they were passing the site of the Tippecanoe Battle Ground, which certainly brought back deep memories for everyone. Just 30 years before, in 1808 Tecumseh and The Prophet had established Prophet's Town in an attempt to unify and consolidate all remaining Indians into a single voice that could be the Indian equivalent of Washington D.C. and the President. It was an attempt to beat the white man using the white man's ways. It was Tecumseh's dream.

And the Indians gathered at this field of dreams—up to a thousand of them by 1811 when General William Henry Harrison gathered a thousand militia to defeat this latest threat of Indian solidarity. Harrison's troops arrived and agreed with The Prophet that there would be no engagement until the next day. Tecumseh was gone recruiting other tribes into his new unified structure. He had left word to not get into any scrapes with the whites, knowing that once all Indians united, the whites would have to make major concessions. Harrison posted a strong guard around the camp in spite of the agreement with The Prophet, not believing the Indian's word. Upon seeing a vision where the white's bullets could not harm the Indians, The Prophet rallied the Indians and sent them into a 4 a.m. surprise attack, which technically can be considered "the next day"—depending on when you consider the day beginning. Harrison's troops were ready. The white man's bullets actually *did* penetrate the attacking Indians.

The Indians chalked up here a defeat in their cause of the scope of what a Gettysburg would later be for the South in the Civil war. The hope of a unified Indian nation strong enough to negotiate with Washington DC on more equal terms died here. The Indians left the battlefield defeated and Harrison took Tippecanoe and later added Tyler too and was elected President. The Indian defeat and retreat in despair must have been a painful memory for the Potawatomi. When Tecumseh finally returned from his recruitment trip there was nothing left—no village, no Indians—just the smoldering ruins of a now-dead dream for one unified nation of Indian peoples somewhat equal with the US Government.

Some of the Potawatomi had fought at Tippecanoe so these travelers might have been recalling the horrors of the battle and their lost friends, and maybe even feelings of betrayal. But the whites would have remembered it too. General Tipton was an officer in the fight so this was an old battlefield of glory for him. Judge Polke had also been there and had been wounded in the fighting. Tippecanoe was a place of deep memories and meaning for both races.

Perhaps this is why they made camp an hour after passing the battleground. They made fifteen miles for the day. What happened next may have been prompted by the memory of Tippecanoe. Breaking open the wagons of supplies, the leaders of the removal distributed dry goods to the Indians: cloth, blankets, calico—it must have seemed like one gigantic birthday party—and not just a little either. The expedition distributed $5469.81 worth of dry goods to the Indians—more than $5 per person, man woman and child—a major giveaway in that day's economy. Did the leaders of the journey choose this day on purpose to shower these wares on the Indians to make a point?

One person died today, a very old woman—the mother of chief *We-wiss-sa*—who was said to be over 100 years old. How exactly does a 100 year old woman handle a forced trek from Indiana to Kansas? Perhaps by dying.

FATHER PETIT headed out of South Bend today (or yesterday), first to go south to Logansport then west along the Wabash trying to catch his congregation. He hoped to catch them by Lafayette. Some of this travel may have been by stagecoach and other by hiring locals to take him the next leg of the journey. The stagecoach line did not run from Lafayette to Danville so he had to ride the stagecoach south to Perrysville, which was further south than he needed to go. Petit would have to make "double days" in mileage for almost a week to catch them.

AS FOR ME my day was happy without gifts of calico. Rising an hour before dawn I walked in the dark, then the grayness that announces the coming dawn and by the time the sun actually rose I was a long way toward Battle Ground where Sharon planned to meet me near Interstate 65. After a weekend together I shall return to the trail on Sunday afternoon and walk into Illinois next week.

By the way, the Tippecanoe Battlefield also has another connection to our story. General Tipton, the leader of the Indiana volunteer militia, had been well known as an Indian-hater. He was now in command of this entire removal of the Potawatomi to the Indiana border. We will reflect more on the character of this man when we get rid of him at he Illinois border, but for now, we should mention that he had apparently amassed enough wealth that he was eventually able to purchase the Tippecanoe battlefield site and give it as a gift to the state of Indiana so they could honor his (and others') bravery forever. When I visited, I honored the great vision of Tecumseh. I would rather honor a great vision that failed than a mean-spirited act of success.

I'VE BEEN THINKING about leaders who disappoint. The Prophet at the Tippecanoe battle had promised the white's bullets wouldn't harm Indians. The Indians trusted the prophecy and bet their lives on it. Too bad. It was hard enough to face the deception of the Europeans. I wonder if it was harder to feel deceived by an Indian leader. The Prophet's prophecy didn't pan out. So I go to bed tonight thinking about all the political and church leaders I've known over the years who deceived their followers—either purposely or maybe "accidentally" because their vision was in error. I've been deceived too.

Road-walking near Tippecanoe.

Day 10 Lagrange Indiana --108 Miles
Sept 13, 1838

Dressed in their new shirts and leggings made from the calico distributed at Battle Ground, the Potawatomi now passed beside Lafayette skirting the north, then west side of the town to return back to the shores of the Wabash River to Lafayette's rival port town, Lagrange. This is not modern LaGrange, but Lagrange, a now-abandoned town on the Wabash River. Here from this then-bustling town they invited a local father-son team of physicians (the Ritchies) to examine the Indians. The doctors reported 106 cases of sickness among the 900 or so Indians. (The actual number of Indians is confusing on this journey. It is sometimes reported as "almost a thousand" and at other times lowers numbers. Some escaped, some were left behind to come later, others died on the way, and new children were born. Most historians now settle for 700-800 as the best over all number.) The official accounting of the emigrating party shows no record of any payment to the Ritchies so I presume they did this work *gratis*. There was an official physician of the emigration, a Doctor Jerolaman of Logansport, but he has not yet showed up (though he was already getting paid). Of all the people involved with this removal I like Tipton the least. Dr. Jerolaman I like second least.

In 1838 LaGrange-on-the-Wabash competed successfully with Lafayette. But, alas, having a good port on the Wabash River would not be enough in the future. When the mighty railroad came through later, it bypassed LaGrange and went through Lafayette. Indianapolis was set as the Capital of Indiana because the surveyors arrived when the White River was flooded and thought it has a deep-water port. Alas, the White River was not navigable after all, and the city could not grow much until the railroad arrived in the 1840's. Two rails replaced deep water as the next criterion for success (later to be replaced by four lanes). But before the railroad came, LaGrange was the boomtown while Lafayette sat and waited. Today Lafayette has the railroad but more important, it has Purdue University. LaGrange has a rusty sign hidden in the overgrowth telling how it went out of existence.

There is a written record of seeing these Indians. Some citizens from Lafayette rode out to LaGrange to see the Indian removal for themselves. Sanford Cox published his mournful description in his 1860 book (which has been recently been reprinted under a new title *Old Settlers*). He and a few others rode horses the eight miles from Lafayette to see the band. He wrote the following: "*It was a sad and mournful spectacle to witness these children of the forest slowly retiring form the home of their childhood... All these [lands, trees] they were leaving behind them to be desecrated by the* *plowshares of the white man. As they cast mournful glances back toward these loved scenes, that were rapidly fading in the distance, tears fell from the cheek of the down cast warriors, old men trembled, matrons wept, the swarthy maiden's cheek turned pale, and sighs and half-suppressed sobs escaped from the motley groups as they passed along, some on foot, some on horseback, and others in wagons—sad as a funeral procession."*

It is not clear if this description was written at the time, or as Sanford Cox remembered it twenty years later, but (forgiving the sophomoric attempt at trying to be poetic) if he did not describe the Indians wholly accurately, what he said was nevertheless true. This was certainly the spirit of the forced removal of these Indians. They were a broken people. A remnant. They had taken on the U.S. Empire and lost. They now depended on the charity of the white man to get their calico and blankets—the ones who defeated them. Once proud and ferocious warriors now begged white people for permission to go hunting for a bit of game. Their white guards forbade them to do so (so far). These poor defeated people marched west to Kansas where they had been told they would have fine houses and tilled land where they could live for the first year with full support from the government so they could get established across the Mississippi. Over there in this Promised Land there were no "states" and this new promising land was actually named on the white man's maps as "Indian Territories." If they only had known that even these Indian territories would make good states too, they might have been less submissive on this journey.

FATHER PETIT was probably headed into Logansport today, traveling as fast as he could to catch his flock. He was still over fifty miles behind the Indians and they were walking more every day. When the Indians walked ten miles he had to travel twenty to gain just ten miles on them. Petit tried to rent a carriage or arrange other fast transportation to catch up. His flock was suffering and they needed him.

AS FOR ME I returned to the route after a day off with my wife and began walking through Lafayette. On Sunday evening as I approached an edge-of-town cross street, I heard the words behind me, "Dr. Drury, is that you?" It was Micah, a graduate student in history at Purdue University who had heard about my walk from Brooks Sayer in Logansport. Micah was on his way to see his girlfriend when he found me on the road not far from her house. His apartment turned out to be right on my route. Later that night I slept on Micah's couch leaving his apartment in the morning before he had his first rollover I suspect.

For my breakfast I had a hot dog at the Ravines golf course where I also did informal research on who plays golf on Monday mornings in Lafayette. I counted 37 golfers in all. There were 34 white males, one African-American and one woman.)

Like the Indians did, I too returned now to the Wabash and the site of LaGrange, moving right past it since I'd heard from Shirley Willard that Linda Klinger had a great restaurant in Independence. I mentally ordered several suppers before being disappointed to find the restaurant burned completely to the ground. I ate supper at the only other business in Independence, Indiana—the Coke machine, where I deposited 50 cents and pressed Root Beer and got a Mountain Dew. With my other two quarters I chose Seven Up and got another Mountain Dew. Shrugging I chugged both Dews, and then walked on with enough caffeine inside me to power my walk to the next state. In an hour I found a shady spot near a creek and I camped and crawled in my sleeping bag by seven o'clock. I wonder how 24 oz. of Mountain dew will affect my sleep.

I'VE BEEN THINKING about weakness and poverty. I like to imagine these Indians marching west as erect proud men and women, submitting to indignities with dignity. I suppose that is true in some degree but it is also true that by 1838 much of the Indian ferocity and pride had been beaten out. They had lost their land and lost the money paid for it. They had taken on the Europeans and lost repeatedly. They had all they needed when they had all the land they wanted. But when the land went under cultivation and the Europeans moved in, land for hunting disappeared which meant they lost their means of livelihood and were at the mercy of the whites around them. All this led to a life of poverty. When I try to imagine the Indians lining up to accept calicos and dry goods I shiver. The picture of white generosity is not what I think of as much as poor bare-footed Indians desperately taking pieces of calico for leggings—and feeling relieved. They were dependant.

Trail marker at site of Chief Winamac's abandoned village

Day 11 – Williamsport, Indiana – Mile 126
Sept. 14, 1838

As the Indians moved west onto the prairies, water became increasingly sparse. Their campsites were determined by water—sometimes at 18 mile distances and at other times only eight or ten miles. Streams were simply dried up. The Indians had been marching for 11 days and they were weary. Walking with scant water, they were likely dehydrated which makes for bleary-eyed listless staggering. Today the journal writer wrote, *"indeed not infrequently, person's thro weariness and fatigue take sick along the route. This occupies much of our time. We place them in the wagons which are every day becoming more crowded."* The removal covered eighteen miles today. During the evening two deaths occurred, with no mention if they were children or the aged, man or women. Just two deaths.

FATHER PETIT was still trying to catch the removal party. He could not find a private coach to hire for transporting his gear and himself ahead so he was left at the mercy of the unsure schedule of the public coaches.

The journal describes the prairie thus: *"passing over a dry and seemingly unhealthy portion of the country."* What does an "unhealthy country" look like? Probably the unhealthy contributor to the Indian's sickness was not how the country looked so much as the water, carrying the invisible Typhoid.

AS FOR ME the "unhealthy portion of the country" was Attica, which was only a mile off my route and announced its unhealthiness with large golden arches lifted to the sky across the bridge. After a "Big breakfast" I talked with a reporter on the phone from Lafayette who promised to send out a photographer that afternoon—"Keep walking on that route" was the instruction, "We'll find you." After saluting the Trail of Death marker at the park in Williamsport (on one of their two "2nd streets") I pressed on toward the state line. By dusk it was cloudy and threatening rain but at tiny Marshfield I purchased several candy bars at the grain elevator for dinner, and washed them down with a couple sodas bought at the only other merchant in Marshfield—a body shop specializing in restoring Corvettes from across the Midwest. "Why locate such a business here at this tiny crossroads?" I asked. "Simple—the wife wouldn't move." That seemed like a good enough reason to me.

As I enter increasingly open prairie lands the farmhouses are further apart. And there are fewer trees and thus fewer places to pitch my tiny tarp-tent. I finally found a tiny slit of trees bordering Possum Creek and prepared for what appeared to be a great rain shower overnight. The reporter and photographer never found me today. That's OK; they interrupt my thinking and my feeling anyway.

I'VE BEEN THINKING tonight about the various solutions to the "Indian Problem." *Right-wingers* back then simply wanted to exterminate all Indians like rats. Their view was, "the only good Indian is a dead Indian." *Left-wingers* called for assimilating Indians into the white culture and religion—"Make farmers out of them." The *moderate solution* was to remove the Indians to the west "Where they can continue their own ways." This "Trail of Death" removal of the Indians was the *moderate* solution of the time! I go to sleep tonight wondering what "sensible moderate solutions" I support today that will sound downright immoral to later generations.

Along the Wabash River

Day 12 – Filthy Stream –near Illinois state line—Mile 136
Sept. 15, 1838

The Indians only made ten miles today, stopping by noon at "an unhealthy and filthy stream" near the Illinois line. Later reports from the leaders of this journey said they drank water from streams where the horses refused to drink—perhaps this was one of those streams. The local folk had reported it was too far to the next water source to make it today so they stopped early—it was still a long haul to Danville, yet stopping so soon probably seemed too short for them, but such is the way of walking in dry country. Supplying water for 900 Indians plus all the militia and horses was no easy task when all they found were trickling streams and still puddles.

The highlight of the day for the Indians was permission to go hunting. The whites allowed 25 of the young Indians to hunt for game. This was the first time such permission was given on the journey so far. While nothing is reported of their success, it is doubtful they would have hunted all afternoon and evening without adding some kind of game to the cooking pots for the night. The Potawatomi were now 136 miles from their homes so the emigration's leaders probably assumed the chances of the young men disappearing and going home were now reduced.

On this day "two small children died along the road." This journey wiped out so many of their young. These two simply gave up and died while traveling. Perhaps the leaders didn't even know about it until they got into camp and the dead bodies were reported. They were getting used to death.

FATHER PETIT was catching up to his congregation. He is just a day behind and their slow progress on this day helped. While the band of Indians did not know where he was, he had the advantage of following, thus he would have known exactly when they had passed each town and could have calculated how soon he'd catch them. He was probably frustrated at the time he was taking to catch up—after all they were now in the next *state*. The stagecoach line went out of the way, and the schedule was not a daily route. He certainly was anxious to catch them.

It is worth noting that every day Chief Menominee did not ride with his people but was forced to ride in the jail wagon. Why? What crime had he committed? His crime: he stayed sober and refused to sell his land to the government. For insisting on his right to continue to own property he already owned by treaty, he was jailed as a criminal and forced to ride as a captive in the jail wagon behind the flag of the militia who had arrested him. The flag representing the state of *Indiana*—"land of the Indians." This would be an excellent point for me to remember this man who was caged like an animal for refusing to sell out.

BIOGRAPHICAL SKETCH OF CHIEF MENOMINEE
There were lots of chiefs among the Indians, so why did Menominee get the impressive statue at Twin Lakes? Because, while they all experienced injustice, his was perhaps the greatest injustice of all.

Menominee was known as the "Potawatomi Preacher." In his late 20's he began preaching. Rev. Isaac McCoy examined him as to his worthiness for preaching. McCoy was founder of the Baptist Carey Mission just across the Indiana line in Niles, Michigan. On the first day in April in 1821, seventeen years before the removal, McCoy recorded Menominee's visit. The Indian claimed he was called by God to preach to the Indians to avoid drunkenness, theft and other evil. Apparently McCoy was satisfied with the interview for he issued a paper attesting to having heard him pray and preach and called all to treat him kindly and accept his ministry—a kind of proto ordination (at least for a Baptist).

Menominee did preach and added a notch to a coup stick each time he delivered a sermon. What did he preach? Total abstinence from alcohol and stealing, commitment to hard work and adopting the white mans' ways of farming. And he called the Indians to become Christians and blend into the new country causing no trouble. In short he spoke for semi-assimilation and a peaceful resolution. He recognized that the acreage required for a hunting lifestyle was no longer possible to have thus the efficiency of farming was the only path to the future for the Indians. What did this get him? Nothing. It got him a trip west in the jail wagon and no money for his land that was taken by force. Menominee wound up with neither land nor the money for it. All he got was a statue more than a hundred years later. This is how it is—the prophets they once killed get the honor posthumously from the great great grandchildren of the prophet-killers.

Menominee was a successful preacher and chief. His village expanded from four to more then 100 cabins and wigwams in the next seventeen years. While no preacher's followers are 100% obedient to the preacher's teachings, many of Menominee's Indians did practice total abstinence and they were successfully planting hundreds of acres of corn in Northern Indiana.

Menominee's ties with the Baptists lasted only thirteen years. In

1834 he invited the "black robes" to establish a Catholic mission at Twin Lakes. Why the switch? The journey from Baptist to Catholic is longer than one from Indiana to Kansas. How did this happen? Actually the tribe had originally been evangelized by Jesuit missionaries a generation before Menominee was even born so the roots were there. The older Potawatomi continued to be devout Catholics in their heart. The tribe had continued the custom of twice-daily prayers "after the fashion of the Catholics" white visitors reported. They continued this practice though they had no missionary priest for more than 40 years. This tribal heritage may have been a factor. Or he could have simply considered the Catholic style a more robust form of Christianity. Or maybe the natural alliances with the French made Catholicism more attractive. For wherever reason, Menominee invited the "black robes' to establish a mission at Twin Lakes.

Menominee's conversion to Catholicism cost him. He had taken his wife's sister as a second wife, which was the custom then in order to care and provide for her. He had asked the Baptist McCoy if he needed to discard this second wife and McCoy thought "it would be like gouging out an eye" so (after a long fast seeking God's leading from which he got no guidance) Menominee kept both wives. However when the first "black robe" priest came (Father Deseille), he insisted on only one wife. Thus, when Menominee was baptized as a Catholic, his first wife was baptized with him and they received a Catholic marriage ceremony. Nothing is reported of the wife he "put off." In this baptism the "Potawatomi preacher" became a devout Roman Catholic.

Menominee's fame today is rooted in his refusal to sign the treaties selling his land to the Government. Most other chiefs did sign these treaties and received payment for the land at $1 acre. Menominee wouldn't sign. He even went to Washington D.C. intent on seeing President Andrew Jackson to defend his right to stay in Indiana. (It is not clear if he got in to see him). But all efforts failed. Father Deseille worked to defend the Indians' rights. But the Father then got in trouble with the government who quickly labeled him a foreign troublemaker. He died before they could expel him. This is how Father Petit got assigned to Twin Lakes—as Father Deseille's replacement.

The Catholic Chief Menominee was still in a jail wagon choked with dust and on parade for all to see at this point in the procession. When they would proceed through each small town one can imagine people responding, "See the Indian chief defeated and jailed and on his way to unknown parts!" His crime: refusing to sell his land to the government. It is this Menominee who has just camped his 12th night near the

Illinois border after another day in the jail wagon, dry and chocked with dust.

As for me I have plenty of water—at every farmhouse there are willing and helpful people happy to help me on my journey. So I pressed on, anxious to get to Danville before the threatening storm that never came last night actually caught up to its reputation. Saluting the daily stone marker I always sit beside, and saying goodbye to State Line City and the Gopher Hill Cemetery and I walked on toward Danville.

I'VE BEEN THINKING now about Andrew Jackson. Jackson was President when these Indian Removals started and continued. He had set out the goal of "speedy removal" of the Indians in his first annual address to congress eight years before this 1838 Potawatomi removal. Menominee was convinced that Jackson would play fair, even though he suspected those around him were unscrupulous. Menominee was wrong. Jackson's mind was made up—the Indians must go. It was the final solution. President Jackson became known as the "hero of the common man." Apparently that did not extend to common men who were Indians.

Feet: The walker's weakest link

Day 13 – Danville, Illinois Mile 151
Sept. 16, 1838

The migrating party left seven sick people behind at the "filthy stream," one of who was about to go into labor. They were to catch up later. The heat and dust distressed the travelers today. The journal writer reported, *"the horses are jaded, the Indians sickly, and many persons engaged in the emigration are more or less sick."* After a fifteen-mile journey they camped near the town of Danville, Illinois, which was a village about the size of the emigrating Potawatomi—about 800-1000. No person was recorded to have died among the Potawatomi today, but the journal writer reported that in the nearby town of about the same size four people died on this day. He says, *"it is worthy of remark, perhaps, that such a season for sickness in this country is almost unparalleled."* No deaths are only one of two great bright points. The other is the arrival of Father Benjamin Petit

FATHER PETIT! He had been gaining on the Indians, but not fast enough for him. Finally he took drastic action. Having gone all the way to South Bend to collect his baggage, he got almost two weeks behind his flock. Now he left this baggage in Perrysville with a Catholic man (M. Young) who offered Petit a horse and accompanied him the rest of the way to Danville where he was united with his congregation. The baggage would have to catch up to him later one way or another.

Petit's Bishop had refused to allow him to accompany the emigration from Twin lakes, believing it might appear the Catholic Church was collaborating with this shameful deed. We remember today how in Logansport the Bishop had relented and given permission for Petit to join his parishioners. Now in Danville, Petit finally caught up to his beloved flock and it was Sunday. The Indians trusted Father Petit.

Seldom has it ever paid for Indians to trust a white man (and never has it paid off for them to trust a white institution). But Petit was a true Christian and a true missionary and he was worthy of their trust from what we read in the story. At least for a white man he was trustworthy. On arrival he immediately went to work. First he prevailed upon Tipton to release Menominee (and the other chiefs) from the jail wagon. Tipton did so, on Petit's word. He may have started arguing for taking Sundays off for a full mass and rest, for this would happen before long. Certainly he went among his people ministering to them spiritually and physically, and he now joined the Indians in their daily morning and evening prayers (which they had continued without him all this time).

When Father Petit first saw his Indians he got a jolt. He spied his Indian congregation traveling ahead of him and it broke his heart. He described this sight in a letter to Bishop Brute this way: *"Soon afterward I saw my poor Christians, under a burning noonday sun, amidst clouds of dust, marching in a line, surrounded by soldiers who were hurrying their steps. Next came the baggage wagons, in which numerous invalids, children, and women, too weak to walk, were crammed. They encamped half a mile from the town, and in a short while I went among them I found the camp just as you saw it, Monsignor, at Logansport—a sense of desolation, with sick and dying people on all sides. Nearly all the children, weakened by the heat, had fallen into a state of complete languor and depression. I baptized several who were newly born—happy Christians, who with their first step passed from earthly exile to the heavenly sojourn."*

General Tipton welcomed the road-weary Petit graciously, even standing up from his chair to offer him a seat, which surprised Petit. The priest's race to catch up with his congregation had certainly wearied him. That night, after completing "a few baptisms" he collapsed to sleep in the tent of General Morgan, his first night in a tent since leaving home. The next morning (September 17) Judge Polke announced that he had arranged to buy a horse from an Indian for the weary and sickly priest to ride. Almost simultaneously the Indian appeared with the horse and said, "My father, I give it to you, saddled and bridled."

It was this young pastor's story that has so captivated me about the Trail of Death. There is plenty of bad to go around in this story. But Benjamin Petit is some of the good that goes around.

FATHER BENJAMIN PETIT

Benjamin Petit did not start out as a priest, but as a lawyer. He prepared for a career in law in Rennes, France and later felt called to become a priest and a missionary to America. He arrived at the Twin Lakes village just one year before their removal. In a single year he learned their language and became their trusted friend. He assisted Chief Menominee in attempting to get the President to relent on the removal but they failed. As a foreigner, Petit had to walk the fine line between condemning wrong and condemning it so stoutly that the US government would send him packing.

One example of this careful negotiating of a political minefield is seen in his letter to General Tipton on September 3, 1838. In Petit's rough draft of the letter he condemns the action stating, *"...to make from free men slaves, no man can take upon himself to do so in this free country. Those who wish to move must be moved; those who want to remain must be left to themselves. ...of course it is against men under protection of the law, that you act is such a dictatorial manner; it is impossible for me, and for many to conceive how such events may take place in this country of liberty."* However, when Petit copied his draft over to actually send to Senator Tipton he omitted this entire scathing paragraph. Since his predecessor priest had been labeled a troublemaker for stirring up resistance against the government, Petit apparently decided to be a priest to the crushed rather than attack the crushers. Whether he made the correct choice or not is debated by every minister and missionary—should they stay at the bottom of the river pulling out bloodied and broken souls to mend them, or go upriver and engage the thing that is doing the bloodying and breaking? Petit did a bit of both. But by the time he joined the expedition in Danville the die was cast, the deed was done. He was downstream now with a bloodied and bruised people and he did his best to bring loving healing and care. He was absent the first thirteen days and 150 miles because he had returned to gather his personal baggage for the trip. He caught them just across the border in Illinois, almost two weeks into the eight-week trip,.

Petit buried the dead, comforted the bereaved, led prayers morning and night, and generally cared for the sick along with celebrating mass each Sunday morning. His calling was to provide spiritual care for his flock and turn them over to a Jesuit father at the Sugar Creek mission in Kansas near the site where the Potawatomi were to be dropped off. The journey was no easy trip for this young missionary. He frequently came down with fever—probably Typhoid. For half of his journey—an entire month—one of his eyes was infected and inflamed while the constant dust clouds irritated this malady. He became increasingly exhausted as he moved west. By the end of the trip Petit's body would be covered with infected boils, some as large as a person' thumb. He would not be able to lie or sit in any position without pain. But even with this personal pain he wrote glowingly about his Indian flock, describing their religious zeal: *"The Indians would attend Holy Sacrifice, during which they astonished the ears of the spectators by singing hymns, some of which—for me at least—had a sweet harmony indeed."*

This missionary priest paid a price to perform his ministry. At this point he was not aware of what that final price would be for his full measure of devotion.

AS FOR ME I walked hurriedly into Danville where a reporter from the Danville Commercial News connected with me for a newspaper interview just as it started to rain. As a reward for walking the first 150 miles, and entering a new state, (but most of all because of the downpour) I got a room at the Days Inn where the night manager allowed me to use their business computer to write this journal late into the night. Tomorrow I go to the post office to collect my mail for the second time. I'm thankful in advance to those who will send a letter to cheer me up. I'll crawl in my tent tomorrow night and read them all!

I'VE BEEN THINKING today about restitution. The Bible teaches the idea of "restitution" –paying back generously for past evil. When the crooked tax collector Zacchaeus encountered Jesus, he promised to right the wrongs he had committed by paying back money he had wrongfully taken, four times over, plus giving away half his net worth to the poor. The idea is Biblical—doing restitution for past wrongs. So do Europeans owe some sort of restitution to the Indians? To what extent does one's race make us guilty? Who stole from the Indians? Who should pay it back? To whom should it be paid? I don't know the answers to all these questions. But I just know God expects wrongs to be righted by someone. It seems to me like the Christian people ought to be in the front of any move for restitution or reparations. Are we?

A Chilly day in May

Day 14-16 Sandusky's Point, Illinois (Catlin) -- Mile 157
Sept. 17-19, 1838

The Indians and their escorts stayed three nights at Sandusky's Point (near present day Catlin) for two reasons. First, the Indiana militia had to be discharged since they were now beyond the state borders and no longer had any jurisdiction. Second was the *"weak condition of many of the emigrants demanding rest."*

On the first day off several of the sick who were left at the "filthy stream" caught up with the column, including a new child who had been born to the woman in labor who had been left behind. However the birth of a new child was countered with the journal entry, *"a young child died directly after coming into camp."* Plus one; minus one.

On their second evening a child and a woman died though they also had another birth. On this day more than two weeks into their eight-week journey, Dr. Jerolaman, the official physician of the emigration finally arrived. After inspecting the Indians he reported 67 sick, 47 of them with "intermittent fever" among other physical complaints. He considered eight "dangerously ill."

On the third day at Sandusky's Point the administrators finished their record-keeping and completed organizing their accounts. The doctor reported not much improvement among the sick, and there continued to be *"six or eight cases as very dangerous."* In the evening a child of six or eight died which was no longer unusual. During the night an adult person also died. The camp quietly buried their dead the next morning before leaving camp—more than 40 Potawatomi were put in graves marked only by crude crosses they could make out of whatever wood they scrounged from near the route, often from an open prairie with scant wood for a fire or cross except along the creek banks.

FATHER PETIT, quickly went about serving as the Indian's priest. While at Sandusky's Point his diary shows he officiated at mass twice on two successive days. His pastor's diary also shows he cared for six deaths and performed two public baptisms and three private baptisms. Perhaps these private baptisms were for the three children who died during this stay. While the official journal records five deaths at Sandusky's Point, Petit records *"we left behind six graves in the shadow of the cross."* The variance between Petit's records and the official journal may be explained by the practice of not reporting the deaths of those left behind or not present with the emigrating party. However another explanation is that so many were dying that the official journal could hardly keep perfect track. Certainly the official record is the minimum number of deaths. Petit presided at many (perhaps most?) of these funerals. He described the usual all-night wakes in a letter to Bishop Brute this way: *"Often throughout the entire night, around a blazing fire, before a tent in which a solitary candle burned, fifteen or twenty Indians would sing hymns and tell their beads. One of their friends who had died was laid out in the tent; they performed the last religious rites for him in this way. The next morning the grave would be dug; the family, sad but tearless, stayed after the general departure. The priest, attired in his stole, recited prayers, blessed the grave, and cast the first shovelful of earth on the rude coffin; the pit was filled and a little cross placed there.* Few duties of a pastor are more heart-rending than performing a funeral for a child—Petit faced this duty almost daily as the emigrating party moved westward.

AS FOR ME I left the Danville Post office in high spirits with a pack of mail. Letters and cards (and sometimes even packets of candy) came from all sorts of people—some I know and many I've never met. Former students like Josh Jackson and Beth Lahni, my wife, Sharon, who faithfully sends clippings and news from home, Larry Wilson my editor, plus a half dozen other folk I've never met who learned about the walk in their local newspaper or at my web site. I read then responded to each person before leaving town. It is the least I can do for people who have been so thoughtful to me.

As I walked the road out of Danville a carload of giggling high school girls slowed down to shout something out the window that was garbled as they giggled. I couldn't make out what they were shouting as they drove laughingly by. Then far down the road I saw them turn around in a driveway and head back toward me. Assuming they might toss out a bottle at me I stepped off the road into the grass. Sure enough, as the car slowed a bit, giggling in unison I saw a window roll down. Out fluttered a scarf. At least I thought it was a scarf. Actually it turned out to be a pair of panties that floating down and landed on the grass at my feet. I could still hear the girls' giggles as their faces filled the back window. I walked past the underpants recognizing that behavior which might be considered flirting to a young man was simply taunting an old man like me. As more evidence of my age, the first thought that crossed my mind was, "Gee, I wonder how much those underpants cost her dad?"

Today I walked into the wind all day, like swimming against a powerful current. In this case the "current" is about 40 mph and I walked leaning toward it as the rain steadily increased through the day. And it is cold—in the

40's with 40 mph wind and raining—the very worst conditions for walking. I'd rather walk in snow than in 40-degree rain. Having only a tee shirt and a windbreaker with me, my body temperature gradually dropped until I could no longer tie my shoes. Finally I found shelter on the leeward side of a farm implement shed pitching my tiny tent I crawled in and went to sleep by suppertime, hoping for a warmer drier day tomorrow.

I'VE BEEN THINKING about the name of this trail today. It is popularly known as the "Trail of Death" because of the high number of deaths—especially children—in the first month walking across Indiana and Illinois. There were plenty of other removals—scores of them in the 1830's alone. Death was also prevalent on those journeys too; on some the percentages were much higher than this one. I admit it is a lousy name for this route. And it isn't a great name for a book either—who wants to read about a "Trail of Death?" The "Trail of Tears" describing the Cherokee removal is so much more romantic. It is a better "sell" to the public. Even white folk can picture an old Indian with tears in his eyes looking back at the land of his fathers as he is prodding forward, tears streaming down his cheeks. What a great movie scene. The "Trail of Death" is not as romantic. And the title focuses on the European's injustice more than the Indian's courageous response. Who wants to read a book piling up more guilt on white males? I suppose I think it would be nicer to call this trail the "Trail of Courage" (as the annual festival at Rochester, Indiana is now called, located near the Trail of Death's originating point). That name would sell more books I bet—everyone likes to read a tale of courage. From my perspective though, I'd love to call it the "Trail of Faith." That would reflect the devotion of the Christian Indians in the face of injustice. But historical names stick. So I'm stuck with "Trail of Death." I've just got to make the insides of this book show more courage and faith than the outside title will.

Day 17 Davis Point, Illinois (Homer) –Mile 167
Sept. 20, 1838

The encampment rose at 3 a.m. in order to discharge the Indiana Militia this morning. By sunrise they had lined them up, marched them to Tipton's headquarters and paid them off, based on the accounting they'd been doing the last few days. Only sixteen of the volunteers would remain. These sixteen would be under the command of William Polk, the federal "conductor" of the emigration.

Here at Davis Point the command of the column transitioned from General Tipton of the Indiana Militia to William Polke, the federal conductor who would escort the Indians the rest of the way to Kansas. This is the point in the story where we bid Tipton farewell—or good riddance depending on your view. So this is a good point in this story to write a short biography and you can decide for yourself.

JOHN TIPTON
John Tipton was an Indian-hater and a military man at heart. At age 23 (1809) he became a member of the "Yellow Jackets" a local militia in Harrison County, Indiana. He fought at the Battle of Tippecanoe with William Henry Harrison when he was only twenty-five years old (1811). He wrote descriptive accounts describing how the Indians broke their promise to not attack. He was able to trade some of his military glory for political gain. He became sheriff of Harrison County and got elected to the Indiana state legislature. He was appointed to the commission to select Indiana's new capital (they chose the tiny town of "Fall Creek" which later was renamed Indianapolis). He divorced his first wife (his cousin) at age 35. He landed the appointment as Indian Agent for both the Potawatomi and the Miami tribes at age 37. At 39 he remarried, this time to the daughter of his best friend, Spier Spencer whom he had watched die at the Battle of Tippecanoe.

Tipton at age 42 moved the Indian agency from Ft. Wayne to Eel River and there he laid out the city of Logansport, Indiana. During his time as Indian agent he negotiated the treaties that got the government land for the Michigan Road and eventually significant lands for white settlers. As we already mentioned, he also personally purchased the land where the Battle of Tippecanoe occurred and gave it to the state. When US, Senator Noble died, Tipton was appointed to replace him, to finish out that term—he was 45 at the time. He was re-elected then at age 46.

When Tipton was 52 Governor David Wallace appointed General Tipton (he held the rank of Brigadier General in the Indiana Militia) to recruit volunteers and swear them into a militia to forcibly remove the Potawatomi Indians from Indiana. Tipton recruited 100 men and marched them to the Twin Lakes village of Menomonee and surrounded the Indians while they were in a council of peace. After he intimidating the Indians into submitting, the captives were force-marched to Kansas where they had been promised new homes and tilled land and a year's worth of government payments to help them get on their feet. While this promise of land was nowhere written down, it was clearly understood by the Indians. In Judge Polke's writings after the party had arrived in Kansas, it is clear the Indians believed they were promised both houses and cultivated land—not unbroken prairie. Who promised this and what they promised we do not know for sure since the government was apparently careful to not include these promises in the written treaties. In a later entry by Polke (November 24) he confirms that General Tipton had promised the Indians a government-built new chapel. It makes one wonder if General Tipton was the promise-maker for the homes and cultivated land as well. Tipton did not have to deliver on these promises—he left the emigration just across the Indiana border in Illinois.

General Tipton may have found glory at Tippecanoe but there was no glory in this assignment. He had been a famed Indian-fighter, but the poor tattered tribe he forced to Kansas was a sad remnant with little fight left—there was no gory in this. His letters about the removal carry no feeling of glory or even hate—just a sense of doing a messy task that most every (white) person thought needed done. He may have hated the Indians at one time, but the worst feelings coming through his letters on this emigration is contempt or scorn for the defeated Indians—his hate had lost its edge. There was no glory for a powerful and triumphant nation to force a remnant band of leftover Indians off their lands at bayonet point. Tipton must have known this. This was a messy thing that "had to be done" according to the Governor, and Tipton would do it. He would get rid of this "Indian problem" once and for all by removing the remnant far from the borders of Indiana.

So was Tipton a bad man? There were reports that he did not even allow time for the Indians to drink along the way but hurried them on before they were finished drinking, using a threatened prick of the bayonet. The Logansport newspaper reported these rumors and denied them, defending their founder and leading citizen. Were they true? I think they were. Any person who has led a traveling group knows how hard it is to get the group to move and how a group tends to lag at every stop. I've led groups of college students through Europe and have experienced the frustration of "one more stop at the bathroom before we leave" then one more, then another, until finally the first person who went to the bathroom has to go again! I've hiked with students who languish at every break stop and the only way to get them going again is to start up and leave them sitting by the stream. I think it is human nature. When people are in large groups, they naturally sit around at every stop until their leader forces them to march on. I suspect at streams when the command was given to move any normal human being (especially while crossing the dusty prairies in 1838) would lag behind to take one more drink. And I suspect that the militia soldiers rode up and shouted, even threatening with their bayonets to get everyone moving again. So I think it happened, though I can't prove it.

Tipton hated Indians but he had some reason. He had a personal history with Indians. When he was just seven years old and living in Tennessee, the Cherokee killed his father, Joshua Tipton. At age seven he had to take on the role of "man of the house" and care for his family. He and his mother moved the family to Indiana when he was twenty-one. How much of his hate came from losing his dad at such a young age? We do not know. We just know he was known for being an Indian-hater. However, it should be mentioned that hating or scorning Indians was in fact the norm for the day. It is this norm, which led to the rise of the term "Indian lover." This term rose to label the person who had the unusual attitude departing from the average opposite collective attitude.

Whatever, General Tipton is not remembered today for the glory of fighting at Tippecanoe. Nor is he remembered for his two terms in the U. S Senate. He is remembered for this shameful deed of forced removal of these Indians from Indiana in 1838 when he was 52 years old. At the time getting rid of the "pesky Indians" may have made him a hero. Today it stains his entire life.

It would be convenient for us to blame John Tipton for this entire injustice. But to do so would let too many others off the hook. Tipton did not act alone. This was no mob action. It was the legal and intentional act of the state and federal governments. Others carry the blame along with Tipton. We cannot get away with saying, "Tipton was a bad man and that is why this happened." Indiana Governor Wallace made the decision to recruit the militia from his safe harbor in the state Capital but his hands are bloodied too. The treachery of Col. Abel

Pepper in using alcohol and deceit to coerce the Indians to sign over land deserves perhaps the strongest moral condemnation of all. But there is also a lengthy list of the forgotten names of all legislators who voted on shameful resolutions that encouraged whites to take land by "pre-emption"—by simply moving onto the Indian land in anticipation of their later sale. The United States Congress must share a heavy part of this shame for what they called their "humane" removal acts forcing Indians across the Mississippi River. And certainly we cannot let the arrogant law-defying despicable President Andrew Jackson off the hook. Nor the hundreds of traders and white immigrants who stood to gain by the Indians banishment. This was not an action of one white man gone bad. It was the collective action of U.S. governments and its people. When a group sins together it is so much harder to bring confession and repentance. Let alone restitution.

AS FOR ME I continued walking into the wind and rain pondering Tipton's life and its lessons as I tried to reach the next campsite at Sidney, Illinois where I hoped to meet Sharon for a weekend off. Maybe the rain and cold will pass while I rest in the Champaign area this Saturday and Sunday.

I'VE BEEN THINKING about Indian life this afternoon. What seduced the Indians to leave their traditional way of life? Why couldn't we both survive with the whites and the Indians dealing with each other with a "live and let live" attitude? It didn't happen. These were not just two races clashing but two ways of life. The Indian lifestyle required vast tracks of land where they could hunt. Europeans had the curious notion of "private property" and expected others to stay off land once they'd fenced it in. As Europeans gobbled up land the Indians were left with few options to feed their children except to become farmers like the whites or hunt on the white's "private property." Settlers thought they were justified shooting an Indian "trespasser." Indians retaliated when one of their people were shot. So the clash of two cultures continued. But that can't explain *this* Indian removal. The Potawatomi had become *farmers* –the had largely left the life of hunting, avoiding the starvation of the winters such a life now brought them, They were Indiana *farmers*. Farmers being forced to leave their own property. Their farmland was in Indiana—land of the Indians! They were not forced out because they were hunters. They were forced out of the state because they were *Indians*.

Day 18 Sidney, Illinois –Mile 179
Sept. 21, 1838

They are on the Grand Prairie now—open country for miles they walked across unbroken sod with only occasional trees clustered in groves or clinging to the banks of creeks and streams. It was hot and the blistering sun caused the dust to billow, chocking the riders, walkers, and especially those in the sick wagons where the canvas tops served to capture and collect the dust. The official journal reports the Indian health *"scarcely a change"* from yesterday with fifty sick in camp and three dying since the last journal entry. Finally they made camp near the present town of Sidney It was *"poorly watered"* and a child died after coming into camp. This morning one of the chiefs died, Muk-kose *"a man remarkable for his honesty and integrity"* states the journal for the day. The journal also reports that forage for the animals was a bit easier to procure and they were occasionally able to purchase some bacon to add to their now-boring diet of beef and flour.

FATHER PETIT recorded two deaths today. His personal diary reads, *"Camp Sidney: 2 deaths—appointed as interpreter."* Since he had learned the language he was about to serve as interpreter. It also put him on the payroll, which may have caused him some misgiving—or perhaps should have? Whatever, he did rounds with the medical doctors to interview the sick and functioned as interpreter in cases where the officers and the Indians needed to communicate. This was no small task—the Potawatomi language is complicated and difficult to acquire. Some missionaries to the Potawatomi never got the language at all and thus gave themselves instead to a life of prayer for the Indians. But Petit applied himself and learned enough Potawatomi to serve as interpreter and even preached some sermons without the aid of an interpreter, which he reported had really delighted the Indians. The notion of destroying Indian culture and language was a method of some missionaries (and especially boarding schools) but it was not the method of Petit. Perhaps his background in the French approach to cultural matters (as opposed to the English approach) is the reason for his enlightened "missiology." The Indians continued to die, one or more every day. But in death they were at least accompanied by their beloved priest. Father Petit would be with them for the rest of the journey.

AS FOR ME I continued to walk until I had recorded a "double day" covering the two day's Potawatomi journey in one day. I walked into Sidney half frozen in the 40 degree wind and rain where Sharon met me at Clancy's gas station, the only "restaurant" in Sidney. I am taking the next day off to sleep at the Drury Inn (appropriately so) at Champaign/Urbana, Illinois. I hear that I may have two companions join me in walking this coming week—at least my phone messages say so—I hope they come; I'm getting bored with myself.

I'VE BEEN THINKING tonight about people who consider themselves "part Indian." When folk find out what I'm doing they often tell me, "You know, I'm 1/16th Cherokee myself." Certainly there are not this many "part Indians," are there? I have only met one person so far who claimed Potawatomi heritage but maybe 25% of the people I talk to say they are "part Cherokee." It is getting humorous and I can see it coming in a conversation now. This sort of thing is a big inside joke among Native Americans. White man says, "I'm 1/16th Cherokee, you know," to which the Native American nods appreciatively as if impressed while at the same time flashing the tiniest grin and flash of his eyes to his nearby Indian friends. The white guy never gets that he is being mocked and continues to tell his family story. Why is it that whites want to be "part Indian?" Do we suppose "Indian blood" is somehow more heroic than white genes? Is it the white way of identifying with the Indian's injustice and suffering? Or could it be some sort of subliminal put-down for Native Americans—that is, white guy is saying under his breath, "I have Indian blood too but look at how successful I am—I rose above it and worked hard and escaped poverty—c'mon, get over past injustice and work hard like me and get ahead" I don't know why they do it but apparently being "part Indian" is cool for many white people. In that case I'm not cool. I am mostly English with a bit of Irish and Scot mixed in and not even 1/32nd Indian. I am walking this route as a white man though I'm trying to capture an Indian point of view as best I can, but I'm not doing that very well I suspect.

Day 19 Sidoris Grove, Illinois –Mile 195
Sept. 22, 1838

Until today heat and dust had been a problem for the Indiana, sbut on the way to Sidoris' Grove the weather turned bitter cold. It was late September when the Potawatomi passed this way. Heavy rain had brought a cold front and they walked sixteen miles from Sidney to the grove of trees at Sidoris on the bitter cold open prairie. In spite of the cold, the official journal assesses the health of the camp improving; *"not a death has occurred to-day."*

Sidoris Grove had been a traditional gathering place for the prairie Indians long before Henry Sidoris settled there fourteen years before the Potawatomi passed this way. Henry drove six yoke of oxen pulling a prairie Schooner to this site. The oxen were strong enough to break the foot-thick sod of the prairie to "turn the land into something useful."

On this day the westward-moving band discharged a wagoner for drunkenness, which meant he had to turn around his wagon and return all the way home on his own, no small punishment. However, the wagoner may not have been from Indiana. One of the challenges Polke contended with was that some of the original wagoners had walked off the job. He had to continually hire new ones as the emigration moved west and it is likely that Polke's son did some of this negotiating along with the purchase of food from farmers along the way. They needed the wagons for the sick. In the evening two Indians became intoxicated and were arrested and put under guard. (They did not discharge and send the drunken Indians back to Indiana, though.) This may be a good point to remember that though Menominee preached total abstinence from alcohol this migrating group included many Indiana not in his band, or some in his band who ignored his teaching. Many followed other chiefs, and who were neither Christian nor Catholic. While I am especially interested in the Christian side of this story as a Christian minister, I do know that some of these Indians were not devout Christians nor Catholics any more than all Americans are Christians today. Besides, to be Catholic is not to practice total abstinence from alcohol anyway—that was a special teaching of Menominee more than the Catholic Church. It might have been an idea Menominee harvested from his connection with the Baptists more than the black robed Catholic priests. So there were other chiefs among this party heading westward. Indeed, General Tipton refused to even consider Menominee a chief, but only would admit he was a "principal man." Because he refused to accept payment for his land, it benefited the government to reject him as a chief—thus he would have "had no rights to the land anyway."

FATHER PETIT recorded a two-word phrase in his diary: *"one death."* That's all—just two words representing the day. With nothing much from Father Petit this might be a good time to insert a description of the order of march for the migrating party. The Delphi Oracle newspaper reported on September 15, 1838, that the line stretched for three miles. On another day Petit had described the order this way: *"The order of march was as follows: the United States flag, carried by a dragoon, then one of the principal officers, next the staff baggage carts, then the carriage, which during the whole trip was kept for the use of the Indian chiefs; then one or two chiefs on horseback led a line of 250-300 horses ridden by men, women, children in single file, after the manner of savages. On the flanks of the line at equal distance from each other were the dragoons and volunteers, hastening the stragglers, often with severe gestures and bitter words. After this cavalry came a file of forty baggage wagons filled with luggage and Indians. The sick lying in them, rudely jolted, under canvas which, far from protecting them from the dust and heat, only deprived them of air, for they were as if buried under this burning canopy—several died thus.*

AS FOR ME I now have two companions with me for the next four days: Phil Woodbury, a retired Physician from Indianapolis, and Jason Denniston, a youth pastor from Fairmount, Indiana. We started out in steady rain, passing through Tolono then on for a stop at the only "store" in Sidoris, one owned by the local entrepreneur who is also the mayor. The "store" consisted of a storage unit that had a coke machine in front. We headed on from Sidoris and a giant thunderstorm came up so fast we got soaked before pitching our tents between two Alfalfa fields. We slept wet tonight.

I'VE BEEN THINKING as I go to sleep in the rain-drenched tent about the Indian annuities. I've met white folk who describe Native American life something like this: "They just sit on the reservations and get drunk all the time on government welfare money—we ought to cut them off the dole so they would have to work for a living, then they'd be a better people." Alcohol is indeed a serious problem for some Native Americans. Many Indians could not resist falling prey to it like they also did to the various diseases and plagues brought from Europe. However, the general population often misunderstands annuity payments when they call them "welfare." Some of this goes back to the purchase of Indian lands by treaty. In some cases our government bought millions of acres of land by offering a tribe an annual annuity payment "as long as the sun shines and the moon rises." These were to be annual perpetual payments for the land our government purchased or they were to be the profits from leasing out grazing rights to millions of acres the government held in "trust" for the Indians. This "rent" was to come to the Indian tribe forever. "Trust" is a bad name in this case since millions of dollars have disappeared somewhere between the rich ranchers who are paying grazing fees and the Indian tribes who were supposed to get their fair share. Thus today's Indian warriors do not carry bows and arrows, but carry law school degrees as they wage a new kind of war for justice in courtrooms where they attempt to get a fair share of what was promised to them long ago. Mortgage payments and lease payments should not be considered "welfare."

Camping with Phil Woodbury and Jason Denniston in a fallow field

Day 20 Pyatt's Point (Monticello), Illinois –Mile 210
Sept. 23, 1838

Father Petit persuaded William Polke to let the group leave late today, which is Sunday. Petit wanted to hold mass first and the Indians resisted being forced to get up long before dawn to first attend church services so they could be ready to leave with the column. Polke, the official federal "conductor" of this journey, was now in charge and General Tipton was gone. Polke seemed more open to requests like this.

After mass the Indians walked across 15 miles of open treeless land until they reached the Sangamon River at Piatte's Point (Monticello, Illinois) where they saw their first trees of the prairie. The doctor gave a report of 40 sick Indians. Two deaths occurred, a child early in the morning and a second on the road to this riverside camp. In a letter to Harris, Judge Polke reported today that he purchased a horse at this river for I-O-Weh, paying $62.50. Since the Indians land was bought at $1 an acre, one can readily see the comparative price of transportation—60 times the value of an acre of tilled (Indian) farmland.

The river must have been a welcome sight to these woodland Indians. They were not accustomed to living on open prairies and thus the next few days as they followed the Sangamon River, they would rejoice at the game and shade. They were in for a treat, insofar as was possible considering the sad cause of the journey.

FATHER PETIT records today "2 deaths." No names, just, "two deaths." A mother or father or brother went to bed mourning tonight. Death is just a statistic unless it is your *own* child who is the corpse.

AS FOR my new partners and me we walked the roads and when a bit of sun came out, we spread out our sleeping bags to dry on a grassy spot across from a farmhouse. The country folk responded by promptly calling the county Sheriff who came and ran our ID's through his system. The sheriff's deputy half-apologized for the landowner's response to what they reported as "doing laundry" across the road from them. When we arrived in Monticello, we found a full grocery store at which I bought and ate two pounds of fresh fruit at the price of $6.04. Then we holed up for several hours at McDonald's waiting for the rain to lighten up. Here an 85-year-old man who watched us from a neighboring table offered his own stories of "running the rails" and living in the Hobo Jungle in the 1930's, assuming we were today's equivalent. Once the rain cleared we walked out of town and camped on the ridge just above the Sangamon River—a river we will follow all the way to Springfield, just as the Indians did.

I'VE BEEN THINKING today about Indian team names. There has been plenty of fuss about naming sports teams the "Indians" or "Braves." Is this OK or not? Some Native Americans resent it. The matter gets even more complicated because some tribes applaud using their tribal name and even sign contracts for its use. What do I think about all this? Would I feel OK about calling a team after other races like calling them the Atlanta Negroes or the Los Angeles Latinos? There are the "fighting Irish" and nobody seems to care about that. Why? But having a "mascot" is even touchier. I wonder how I'd feel if a team had a mascot all dressed up like a black slave who leaped about the sidelines. Or how about if another team dressed up their mascot like the Virgin Mary and called themselves the "Madonna's." I suppose I'd consider this invading sacred territory. So, why do white people like to name our teams *savages* or *Indians*? Is it because we want to appear ferocious and these names recall a time when the Indians instilled fear in the hearts of settlers? We tend to do that with animal mascots too I suppose. We call our teams the lions, or tigers, or eagles and bears rather than doves, lambs, kittens and turkeys. We name our teams after powerful and admirable things. I suppose one might argue we would be complimenting lions and bears or the Virgin Mary (thus Indians) when we name our teams after them. But that isn't exactly how it works out, is it? What do I think? I think that if using their racial or religious name offends a group we ought to find another name. Frankly, I'd be caught doing a tomahawk chop even if I lived in Atlanta—ever.

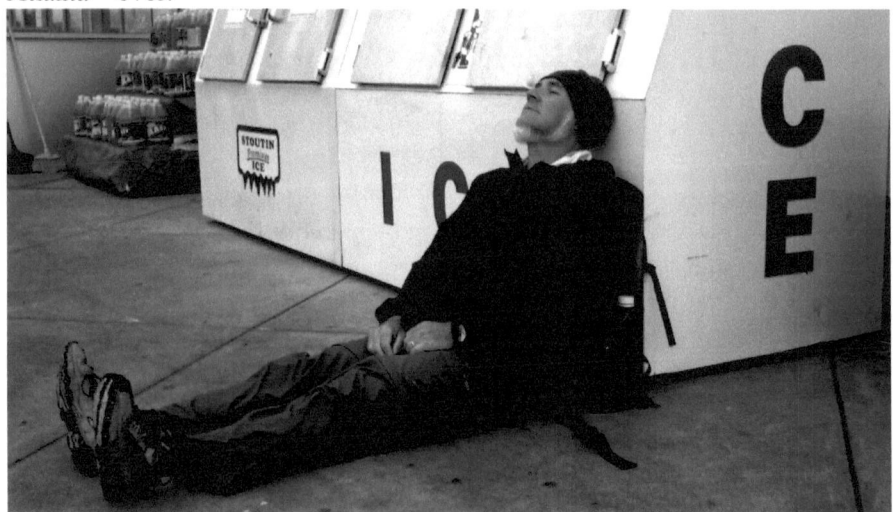

Day 21-22 Sangamon Crossing, near Oreana, Illinois –Mile 225
Sept. 24-25, 1838

The Indians now walked downstream 15 miles along the banks of the Sangamon River where game was plentiful and they walked in sweet shade from the burning sun. They had left 29 sick people behind at Piatt's Point (Monticello, Illinois) who were to catch up to them later. Two people died today as they passed downstream. On the second day when they stayed at this camp another two died: a sick woman from the group left behind died just as they caught up, and a child died in the evening. That totals four deaths here at the crossing. In spite of the previous hopeful entries, the journal writer now states, "*So many emigrants are now ill that the teams now employed are constantly complaining of the great burthens imposed upon them in transporting so many sick.*" The standard procedure was to let the sick ride in wagons.

The great joy for the Indians was being permitted to go hunting. They brought in a "*considerable quantity of game.*" Indeed, along the Sangamon River they would hunt daily to the delight of both the Indians and their white escorts. The wagons spent the second day reloading and redistributing the loads in the wagons after the river crossing.

The migrating party stayed two days here at the Sangamon crossing to allow the sick they'd left behind to catch up and rest a bit at this most delightful place they had not encountered since "Pleasant Run" back along the Wabash River in Indiana. On this day's entry is a report that the doctors were also sick and had been the last several days. However the weather was delightful and they seemed cheered by the country being more thickly settled—at least the white men who wrote the journal were cheered.

FATHER PETIT apparently stayed behind at camp when they left. He entered in his diary, "*remained at the camp called Sangamon Crossing—3 burials. I rejoin the emigration 16 miles further on with the sick, one woman dead on the way*".

AS FOR ME the journey along the river was a welcome treat—sweet shade, chirping birds, a dozen deer and peaceful roads reminding me too of my walk along the old towpath road back at the Wabash River. My companions are wonderful company and we looped out of our walk for a breakfast-lunch-snack at Judy's diner at Cerro Gordo, including several hamburgers each and some fresh pie as we wondered how this town got the Spanish moniker "Fat Hill." Our bellies filled we walked with fresh energy to cover the emigration's next day's miles as well. I am especially motivated to get to Decatur where I am supposed to get a pair of New Balance shoes so I can dump the present Solomon shoes in the nearest trash bin. My Solomon shoes are making hamburger out of my feet and I already regret switching several days ago when I somehow thought I'd give my feet a break from trusty New Balance sneakers. Sharon has sent the faithful NB shoes to Decatur.

I'VE BEEN THINKING today about the connection between black slavery and the Indian removals. The abolition movement was getting some powerful steam when these Indians were being forced out of Indiana. The founders of my own denomination (The Wesleyan Church) were fighting to get their denomination (Methodists) to condemn slavery as sin. The Methodists refused, attempting to keep the north and south together in one denomination at any price. Just five years after the 1838 Potawatomi removal, these Methodist abolitionists would leave the Methodist church and found a new denomination that condemned slavery in no uncertain terms. This was more than twenty years before the Civil War and there were still a great number of states arguing that human beings (if they were black) could be bought and sold like horses and made to work all their life for whoever owned them. I wonder what the founders of my denomination thought about these Indian removals. They rightly condemned the injustice of slavery. But what did they say about the injustice of the Indian removals? Anything at all? Did they consider human slavery so much worse than human removal that they "set priorities" in their social outrage? Or, did they condemn both and just focused their primary energy on what they considered to be a worse sin? Then again, they may have considered removal of the Indians the "moderate solution" as most did at the time. After all, it would be several decades until similar "moderate people" would hatch the idea of founding the African country of Liberia in order to send back there the newly released slaves. Maybe I ought to ask myself tonight, "On what injustice today am I being strangely silent while I fight against what I consider to be worse evils?"

Day 23 Near Decatur, Illinois --239 miles
Sept. 26, 1838; May 17, 2006

The Indians traveled 14 miles today down the river, camping just outside of Decatur. The doctors were still sick so no official report was made on sickness but the journal-writer says, *"the sick appear to be somewhat recruited."* A child died after dark this day.

AS FOR ME my own migrating party of three walked a "double day"—covering both their journey the day before (to the Sangamon Crossing), then walking their next day's miles almost to Decatur. I got to see my first funnel cloud today! I have lived in the Midwest since 1972 and have hoped to see one for years. Today I got my wish. It never touched down but made an impressive elongated spiral in the sky. Finding an abandoned railroad grade we pitched our tents lined up long ways looking forward to a break in Decatur. We took turns listening to the repeated tornado warnings on our tiny radio until finally the warnings were lifted and we fell asleep. The night was more interrupted by the eight railroad trains passing on the occupied tracks twenty feet from our heads than the storm, though several times though the night we recalled the notion that "a tornado sounds like a freight train roaring by."

I'VE BEEN THINKING today about casinos, gambling and modern Indians. When the Seminoles in Florida won a ruling in 1979 that the government had no business regulating gaming on their tribal land (since they were technically a "nation") the door was opened for a multi-billion dollar industry for modern Indians. Soon casinos sprang up and millions of dollars came to poor tribal families. The way gambling works for Indians is dull-witted mathematically challenged white people who have extra money travel to the reservation and leave the money there for dividing between the casino operators and the Indians. Or, at least it is supposed to work that way. Then again, as always, when Indians come into money, the whites quickly show up to rake in millions themselves as they "help" the Native Americans. This would include Jack Abramoff and a hundred other unknown white trash. They followed the Indian emigration in 1838 and they follow them now. As is sometimes the case, tribal elders also can skim off a cut for themselves. But generally gambling has been a boon for the Indians. Is it fair recompense for past injustice—a sort of restitution by legal loophole? It won't last. And, hasn't. Seeing the huge profits available from riverboat gambling nearer home (where white governments could tax the profits and get the jobs) soon lots of competition emerged and has flowered. Why drive (or fly) to an Indian reservation to gamble when you can just run down to French Lick, or

St. Louis. Eventually governments joined the competition directly and went head to head with Indians as they got in the lottery business themselves—as a *government*! Sure enough, when the Indians come onto something profitable, someone shows up to take it away from them. About the only way the Indians can win this is to make sure they have nothing at all the white man wants. This is what sending them to Kansas was supposed to do. What white man would even want this useless land they were headed to in Kansas?

George Winter sketch of the emigration

Day 24 Long Point, Illinois –Mile 253
Sept. 27, 1838

Continuing down the river the Potawatomi passed through Decatur as the Indians continued to *"scour the prairies in search of game."* They were successful. The quantity of venison was so great the leaders did not have to issue rations of beef and flour. The journal puts it *"the camp is now full of venison."* One of the assistant conductors left the group today sick, turning back to Indiana. He was not replaced. Water was plentiful and the leaders were encouraged that the future might improve. Even forage for the horses was less difficult to procure from the roadside farmers. With a feast of venison to enjoy and nobody dying on this day the journal-writer seemed encouraged. There was no official report from the doctors, but many were still sick. They camped today at long Point (near present Niantic) after 14 miles of walking.

AS FOR ME I ate a big breakfast of something besides venison, though I could not identify it for sure, then found a Laundromat where I could fluff up my sleeping bag and dry out its constantly increasing sogginess due to the rain. Then I walked into downtown Decatur for a long interview with the newspaper that featured the story in Friday's paper including a wonderful map and picture thanks to Alicia, the excellent reporter.

I gathered a pile of mail at the Post Office, and unceremoniously dumped my Solomon shoes in a garbage can at the city park. I thus consummated my remarriage to my original New Balance sneakers full of regret I even left them in the first place for these fancy younger Solomon shoes. By evening I had reached Long Point/Niantic, where Michael McNamer (pastor of the local Wesleyan Church) found my two companions of the last fours days and he hauled Phil and Jason back to their car, which they had left at the Sidney post office at the beginning of this week. I shall miss these friends. They joined me on a wet and cold week. I suspect I have some hotter days ahead of me though. Finding the stone marker in Niantic I walked west out of town until I found a tiny corner of a wheat field where I could put up my tent without harming the crop. For four nights I have had lots of conversation and friendship and sharing memories of other walks and trails. Tonight is quiet except for the occasional howling of the various farm dogs providing accountability to each other by howls and barks through the night. I went to sleep reading my mail.

I'VE WAS THINKING today about land ownership. The Indians had a totally different idea of land ownership than the Europeans did. Europeans accepted "individual property rights" and private ownership along with deeds and inheritance of land. Indians had "territories" which were established and defended by war or negotiation but were considered tribal lands. No individual Indian considered that he personally "owned" land when the whites arrived in America—the tribe possessed the land and the Indians used it. There were no deeds or property lines or fences or the notion of "trespassing" on personal property, but all these concepts applied to what was known as tribal territories. These territories were established and defended by war. How would such a European "buy" land from an individual Indian? They would have to deal with the chiefs who would have to represent the tribe. Just like all government leaders, sometimes these chiefs represented the best interests of the tribe and at other times they also represented their own best interest. European systems were constructed around individuals more than tribes and thus catered to rewarding individuals more than groups. They intended to turn Indian tribal culture into an individual competitive culture. In some cases they succeeded. At other times they failed. There are Indian tribes today that hold land as a tribe and individuals use it while other tribes or bands hold land individually "just like the white man." Which is better for the Native Americans today? I can't say. I guess they will have to answer that.

Sangamon Crossing

Day 25 Sangamon Crossing #2, Illinois –Mile 271
Sept. 28, 1838

After 18 miles the Potawatomi now reached their second Sangamon River crossing a few miles before they would enter Springfield, the first really major city on their route. The federal conductor of the "emigration" Judge Polke, asked Chief I-o-weh to get the Indians to dress up to make a snazzy appearance as they passed through this town. The official journal expected that they would *"present quite a gaudy appearance"* to the city folk. To get them to dress up fancy, they were promised some tobacco, something they had been wanting for days.

This would be their last camp on the pleasant Sangamon River. Douglass journaled that they expected there would be a greatly reduced number of sick once the doctors quit being sick themselves and could check on the Indians again. However, in spite of this cheery entry, two children died during the night. What must it be like to wake up in the morning to find your child dead, right beside you in your tent?

AS FOR ME I walked a hard and quiet day. My companions were now gone which makes it seem quieter and the 85 degree heat makes it harder. I walked from one town of 500 to another. In Illiopolis I had breakfast at a tiny diner and answered all the mail I received at Decatur while listening to the conversations of the local farmers and other complainers at the next table. As each farmer left, the group would commence a roundtable critique of his farming actions, his driving or the way he was unable to control his sons. I suspected the farmers knew this, for they all seemed to want to be the last one to leave.

I hopped from one tiny town to another until I was wonderfully rewarded in Buffalo, Illinois where the friendly postmistress steered me to the only store in town—B & D grocery who offered the best meatball sandwich I've had in my life. It was piled high with onions and cheese and I ate it along with drinking a quart of chocolate milk across the street in the perfectly manicured "Buffalo Park." How this walk has made me appreciate public parks, benches, and especially pavilions (as they have here). Automobile travelers can always drive on ten more miles for a place to stop—that's a half-day's journey for me.

An hour or two later I began being seasick. I had a hot 85 degree afternoon sun blazing down with a quart of chocolate milk sloshing about in my stomach and all seven meatballs from the sandwich seems to be floating in the warm chocolate milk—well, you get the picture. I lay down in a shady spot and groaned for several hours. In that time my stomach came to "deal with" the chocolate buttermilk meatball stew and I began to feel better. By dusk I was able to walk again and I walked on to the Sangamon River where I discovered to my dismay that the bridge was completely out. I took a bypass road and spent the night on the flat ground under a cell phone tower and next to a local model airplane club's "airport."

ON THE MORNING OF SATURDAY MAY 20 I walked the 3 or 4 remaining miles into Springfield where I took a three-mile "side trail" to another Drury Inn where I plan to stay two nights picking up my journey again Monday refreshed and scrubbed clean. I also need to write a short biography of my favorite white man on this journey--the federal conductor, William Polke.

ON SECOND THOUGHT, after one night in a smoking room which is all they still had open, and which did not improve the cough I've had since Thursday night, I decided on Sunday morning to "walk on" catching a worship service on my way out of town. It's funny...when hiking I almost always sleep so much better in a tent than in a hotel... looking forward to a better sleep tonight in my tent again. (That's no slight to Drury Inn--if you're gonna' stay in a hotel they're the best!)

WILLIAM POLKE

Like General Tipton, William Polke, the federal conductor of this "emigration" had a negative experience with Indians as a child. However, different from Tipton, Polke chose to let the experience turn his hart *toward* the Indians rather than away from them. He became a friend of Indians--at least as much as any white man was in those days.

Polke was born in (what is now) West Virginia but moved west (as many imaginative whites did in those days) down the Ohio River to Kentucky in 1780. One day while Polke's father was gone, Indians attacked and killed many of the families in the "station" where several families had gathered for safety. On the last day of August in 1782 little seven-year-old William Polke was captured along with his mother and two sisters. The Indians force-marched about 30 survivors north completely across Indiana to Detroit--a "forced emigration" of the whites in this case.

During the march to Detroit William Polke's mother gave birth

to a fourth child. On this trip the Indians adopted little William and he learned their language and by the end of the journey essentially had forgotten English.

When Polke's father came home and found his family gone, he recruited others and set about to recover them. Thirteen months later, on Christmas Eve in Detroit, he was reunited with his family and William learned to speak English all over again. Yet this experience did not turn Polke bitter, but turned him toward the Indians.

William Polke fought with "Mad" Anthony Wayne at age 17 and at age 33 he became an associate judge in Knox County--hence his nickname thereafter, "Judge Polke." He was the interpreter for General William Henry Harrison and Tecumseh at Harrison's house in 1910. The next year, 1911, he had fought and was wounded at the battle of Tippecanoe. He was a member of the Constitutional Convention that wrote the Indiana State Constitution in 1816 and served five terms as state senator. He ran for Lt. Governor of Indiana in 1822 and came in second.

His life had taken a sharp turn at age 49 when he became a missionary and began teaching Indians at Niles Michigan with his brother-in-law, Rev. Isaac McCoy. He continued this work for two years. He was appointed a superintendent for building the Michigan Road and was the first white settler in Fulton County—founding the village of Chippeway, the location of the first campsite of this emigrating party. He had built the first frame house (called the "white house") which is still on the grounds of the Fulton Country Historical Society—the "round barn place" on present day US 31 about ten miles south of the Menominee statue.

His wife, Sarah was known as a friend of Indians. They would leave freshly killed dear on her doorstep as payment for helping their sick. She was considered a devout Christian and was remembered as having memorized the four gospels and the psalms (though this is probably stretched by those who reported—it probably *seemed* like she knew these to others).

In 1838 when the nation needed a federal "conductor" to lead the "removal" of the Indians, they put "Judge Polke" in charge. Once General Tipton escorted the Indians to the state line, Polke took over. It was an injustice—this entire affair. But when something evil is going to be done, at least you hope for a good man to do it. Polke was such a good man. The Indians trusted him. He was wise and fair. In other removal stories the leaders may have intentionally attempted to "let nature execute" the Indians. Not in this journey. While many died, and the trip has been referred to as the "Trail of Death" Polke cannot (in my opinion) be accused of dire evil considering the day. William Polke was 63 when he led this trip—two years older then I am as I retrace their trip.

William Polke was a good man who did an evil deed the best way possible. This is no strange assignment for anyone in leadership.

AS FOR ME, today is Sunday and I'm moving west after a great visit with Gary and Judy from Decatur who rode over on their way to attending an Indian Methodist church. We had breakfast together--wonderful people who were former missionaries to Mexico and now attend either Afro-American churches or Native American churches. I attended a Roman Catholic Church as I have often tried to do on this trip—a tribute to Missionary Petit of sorts and some sort of statement I'm making to myself on this journey about solidarity with other Christians on the core doctrines of Christianity—the Apostle Creed kind of beliefs. The church was jammed with only few seats open. After the service I continued west.

I'VE BEEN THINKING about good people doing evil things a better way. What would I have done if I'd lived near Menominee's village in 1838? I think I'd have fought against removal, but once the federal government passed the laws what would I do? Would I have taken to the streets and led civil disobedience? Would I have made a "hiding place" and tried to rescue some Indians from this fate? Would I have started my own newspaper and fought against the injustice—even if nobody bought the newspaper except a few rich Quakers out East? What would a good man have done back then? Or would I have offered to lead the march hoping to minimize the damage done in the process? I don't know what I would have done. Is it "good" to get involved in a bad thing in order to minimize evil? Or is the "better good" to do nothing at all? In the movie *Schindler's List* this was Schindler's question.

Day 26 McCoy's Mill (Riddle Hill), Illinois—Mile 288
September 29, 1838

The migrating party made a scene in Springfield, the new capital of Illinois. Promised tobacco for their best behavior, the Indians dressed and *"arranged themselves into a line with an unusual display of finery and gaudy trumpetry, marched through the streets of Springfield."* The citizens completely crowded the streets so that it hampered the Indian's progress. They saw how a neighboring state had handled "the Indian problem" and seeing the Indians in fancy dress was their entertainment for the day. Right down town and through the Capital's square they marched. To us today this was a demeaning act—like using children for entertainment in church programs might be considered in the future. But perhaps at the time it was not so objectionable to either the Indians or the whites? I don't know.

The Indians would have seen the impressive new Capitol under construction already for a year now. More in line with Greek construction style, Illinois raised a mighty stone building no match for the natural Indian wigwams. It was a sign of the future. The new owners of this country would build great stone Capitol buildings, skyscrapers, Interstate highways, and go to the moon. We would also introduce big box stores and traffic jams in the coming years. The simple life of the Indians would become a minority sidetrack in a culture of BIG. The Indians would come to be observed like antiques or the Amish.

Did 29-year-old Abraham Lincoln see this parade? He had moved to Springfield a year before and lived only a few blocks from the city square. Perhaps. Or he may have been out practicing circuit-riding law in one of the county seats around Illinois at the time. Whatever, it was a citywide spectacle that day. As a sidelight, just nine years later from this same city square the ill-fated "Donner party" would leave for California. Here in comfortable Springfield our intermittent physician, Dr. Jerolamon, requested permission to stay behind to "recuperate"—the late-arriving doctor was still sick, and still on the payroll.

After marching through Springfield the Potawatomi camped a half dozen miles past the city at McCoy's mill (near present day Riddle Hill) where a marker is found in front of the New Salem United Methodist Church. The journal calls the creek east of the church a stream *"affording little water."*

AS FOR ME I checked all the Lincoln sites then moved west. At

Springfield I saw Lincoln's home and offices (which were not yet occupied at the time of the Potawatomi emigration). I stopped at the marker on the square and read it too, then headed out of town. I'm in my fourth week of walking now so a sort of *westward drift* has settled in—less goal oriented and less scheduled, just constantly drifting west less concerned about distance and mileage. I pitched my tent in a grassy spot overlooking a new millionaire "gentleman's farmhouse" under construction but not yet occupied.

I'VE BEEN THINKING about immigration. The news and radio talk shows are packed this week with talk about the "Mexicans" in our country illegally. It is the conversations in all the diners too. The general feeling of the white folk is these "illegals" ought to be sent back to Mexico and we ought to build a fence to keep others out. This whole discussion strikes me badly while walking and thinking about this Trail of Death. For almost a month I have been following the trail of the original true occupants of this land. Every single white European in my county is an "immigrant." They didn't ask permission to enter this Indian land. If there had been an Indian fence at the east coast at the time, they would have climbed it. Or, more likely, blown it to smithereens with canons. These immigrants drove the original occupants off the land and by hard work "made something of this country." Now they want to shut the spigot off? On this walk it sounds so ludicrous!

Old Capitol in Springfield, Illinois

Day 27 Island Grove, Illinois—Mile 294
September 30, 1838

The Potawatomi only went six miles this day, camping at the idyllic "Island Grove." For whatever reason here and there on these vast open spaces of prairie there were "islands" of great groves of trees watered and shady—such was "Island Grove" as was Sidorus Grove before. The next water was another 10-15 miles which would have made for a 20 mile day, a distance that may have killed off more Indians than were already dying, so the emigration stopped at only six miles today.

The journal recorded a doctor-less report *"health of the sick still improving"* it also recorded *"the death of a child occurred a few hours after encampment."* It is interesting how many of these children apparently survived through the day, and then would expire once they got into camp. In many cases Father Petit would preside over their funeral at night or in the morning before the Potawatomi would move westward again. While there are large stone boulders and bronze plaques marking this route I'm following, but the real markers are the unmarked graves of more than 40 people who died along the way, mostly children. I have visited all these markers so far on this trip, and I am grateful for the people who voluntarily put up the money for them. This is not a government project but a private one—mostly driven by the energy of Shirley Willard in Rochester, Indiana, though there are several score of Boy Scouts and donors who have made them become a reality. I stop at them all, and they are wonderful for attracting attention to the historical event. And they are delightful for anyone touring the Trail of Death in a car—they provide a perfect place to stop, get out, and reflect on that full day's journey that only took 20 minutes to drive in an automobile. For me, however the trail itself is the "sacred place." I am walking only as fast (actually often slower) as the Potawatomi, so every step I take I am reflecting on the journey so that stopping at the markers is more of a rest stop for me. But I hope nobody reading this story that has sponsored markers will feel slighted for this. I appreciate their work and contributions and salute them for it. I suppose nobody who has driven this journey will understand this. Sooner or later another will walk the path and *they* will understand. Will it be *you*?

The Indians were still bringing in "large quantities of game sufficient for their subsistence" so the government was saving money on issuing rations. It is ironic: the Indians now saving the government money in their own forced removal. No matter—they enjoyed both hunting and eating the wild meat better than the standard beef and flour rations given to them by the government. Today a soldier was also dismissed for intoxication the record stating, "*nothing of the kind is permitted.*" It was important that the militia not get drunk when the leaders of the emigration wanted to keep as many Indians from intoxication as they could. They had already dismissed a driver of a wagon for drunkenness, now one of the militiamen was dismissed and would have to take the long trip back home to Indiana alone.

AS FOR ME I drifted past Island Grove since getting water was not my problem. Getting food was. My last food was yesterday in Springfield so I kept looking forward to a gas station on the "Old Jacksonville Road" …all day long, the next 23 miles I looked but got none--not even a soda machine. Each house I knocked at was empty--the farmer was out on the field and the spouse teaching school or working at a factory. I could not even buy a can of beans. I knew this is one risk of my "living off the land" approach to this walk—sometimes I have to go hungry, that was supposed to be part of the experience. It is a part I don't care for. By late afternoon I was quite hungry. I found an unopened pack of gum along the road and chewed all five sticks for the sugar value. The sugar boost didn't last.

Finally, after 20 miles and a day and a half without food a pickup truck stopped. A man in his 30's with odd beads of perspiration all over his face said, "What you up to?" I told him and he asked, 'How can I help?" I suggested if he had anything to eat it would be great and he promptly gave me three sticks of red licorice and a Mountain Dew. I profusely thanked him and he responded with a pained look in his eyes, "Would you pray for me— I'm on my way to the Psychiatrist—they just can't get my medicine right." I did pray for him aloud right then, and when I said "Amen" he reached out and grasped my hand saying, "Thanks—I needed that."

I went to a grassy spot beside the road and laid out my three course dinner, savoring one stick of licorice at a time washing them down with Mountain dew and no Outback steak had ever tasted so good to me. If the fellow had showed up again I would have squeezed *his* hand and said, "Thanks, I needed that." Renewed with energy, I walked the rest of the way into Jacksonville. (My overnight stay in Jacksonville is on tomorrow's entry for it is more relevant to that theme.)

I'VE BEEN THINKING about the image of God. I've done plenty of walking in the forest and on the mountains. People are always saying to me, "I bet you feel closer to God out there in all that beauty." I don't. Actually I feel a greater presence of God on this road walk than I ever sensed in the Rocky Mountains or the Sierra Nevada. Why? The answer is theological. The mountains and streams are not created in the image of God; humans are.

While nature gives some tips about God's character, it is easier to see an image of God in another human being. Humans, not mountains, were created *Imago Dei*. Every day I see in other human being's concern, compassion, mercy, generosity glimpses of the character of God. Why do we imagine God is more present when humans are more absent? After all, for a Christian the greatest revelation of God did not come in a mountain—but in a human being, Jesus Christ. I've decided that after this hike is over I'm going to concentrate daily on watching for God's character in his crowning creation—human beings.

Wolf and Ann-Marie Fuhrig in Jacksonville, Illinois

Day 28 Jacksonville, Illinois Mile 311
October 1, 1838

What is it that makes one city a place of hospitality and another one of hostility? Why are some towns suspicious of outsiders while others open their arms? Or families? Who knows, but Jacksonville was such a town of hospitality in 1838. Leaving Island Grove the Potawatomi traveled to a spot just outside of Jacksonville to camp. During the day two more Indians escaped. One wonders who and why. Was it two braves intent on returning to Indiana? Or was it a young couple—husband and wife or young lovers, who snuck away to blend into the local citizenry and their heirs are now mayors and senators? We don't know, the journal simply states, *"to-night some of the chiefs reported two runaways, who left this morning."* The name "Trail of Death" arose especially because of the greatly reduced number of Indians arriving in Kansas from those who left Indiana. It was originally thought by some that the death rate was over a hundred, maybe even 200. But runaways constantly reduced the number in the party and the best estimate now is that probably 42 people died, mostly children. But that is not to dismiss even that number—the death rate of twenty people per month out of 1000 is enough to wipe out the entire population in a few years, so 40 deaths is a tragedy just the same. And, when it is *your own* child, even a single death can never be dismissed.

This day had brought just such a tragedy. A little girl, a member of Chief Metteah's family, had fallen and been crushed under the wheels of one of the wagons. She had not yet died by the time they arrived at the campsite outside Jacksonville. Imagine the parent's grief. Did they blame themselves for not holding on to her more carefully? How did they feel as their little daughter lay groaning in their tent about to die?

This is where Jacksonville's hospitality emerged. As darkness settled the Indians heard *music*. The Jacksonville town band had gathered and marched to the edge of camp to serenade the Indians. The music might have been a soothing melody for the grieving parents—and for all the Indians. Why did the band come? Who suggested the idea first? Was it like the movie, *It's a Wonderful Life* – a single person made a difference by saying, "Let's go out and serenade the Indians?" We don't know. We just know they did it. I wonder if it brought some Indians to tears?

But that would not be all to the story. The next morning (October 2) Jacksonville would show even more hospitality.

FATHER PETIT may have gotten sick again in Jacksonville. But he refused to stay behind again. He reported to his Bishop: *"A few days before the Illinois River I was stricken with fever. An old Frenchman came to the camp and made me promise, by force of his pleading, to take a few days rest at his home. The next morning he introduced his wife. He had brought his carriage to take me away, but the fear of again finding myself behind the emigration and the difficulties of rejoining it made me reply with a definite refusal."*

AS FOR ME Jacksonville showed me a similar kind of hospitality 158 years later. Wolf and Ann-Marie Fuhrig had contacted Shirley Willard back in Indiana offering to host my stay in Jacksonville. Wolf picked me up at the city square near the Potawatomi memorial. I soon found myself gobbling up an all-you-can-eat pasta dinner at the restored train station in Jacksonville with five PhD's ranging in field from theater to German to American history. The gathering included both the president and vice president of the county historical society. After my last three-licorice-stick meal this was an inviting fill-up! But the conversation was even more delightful than the food with one after another person filling in the local history as it related to the 1838 removal. It turns out Jacksonville has a long history of hospitality. The Potawatomi incident was not an anomaly. I heard the fascinating story of thousands of persecuted Portuguese Presbyterian Protestants who also were received with hospitality when they fled their country. Perhaps a collective attitude of either hospitality or hostility to outsiders breeds and multiplies? I surely benefited. I spent the night in Wolf and Ann-Marie's back yard sleeping on their soft grass. They had offered an inside bed but I now prefer the grass.

I'VE BEEN THINKING about how values change. I know some Native Americans will reject my description of Jacksonville. After all, having Indians dress up and parade around town with the promise of tobacco would be a terribly humiliating thing to do today. But then was not now. In 1838 black families were sold and bought as slaves in half our nation and they would be illegally lynched—even in Marion, Indiana—for another hundred years. Men shot other men on the frontier without much fear except from the friends of the dead man. Women lived lives of drudgery not much better than slaves, often dying in childbirth so that many frontier men "went through several women" in a lifetime. It would be almost a century before women would be allowed to vote. We modern folk like to imagine the past as better than the present. It was seldom so. Viewed in that context, the dressing up of the Potawatomi may be less humiliating. Though, I agree that in today's world it is, and Indians are still used today to "dress up and dance for the white audiences" in some places. The question for me is, what am I doing or saying today that will *some day* be considered humiliating?

Day 29 Exeter, Illinois Mile 327
October 2, 1838

In the morning as the Potawatomi passed through Jacksonville the town band came out to lead them. They arranged with Judge Polke for the band to lead the Indians into the city square *"where they remained for fifteen or twenty minutes." Presents of tobacco and pipes in abundance were made by the citizens to the Indians."* How did this happen? Who suggested it? Who hatched the idea of presents? Who spread the idea around the night before and in the morning? Incidents like these seldom "just happen" –somebody thinks of the act of kindness and then speaks up. When the Potawatomi marched through Springfield they got tobacco from the federal conductor as pay-for-good-behavior (and for dressing up). In Jacksonville they got tobacco and pipes as gifts directly from the Jacksonville citizens. What a tribute to these folk. And here we are remembering their hospitality 158 years later.

Today they would make 16 miles to Exeter on a warm and dusty day with scarce water along the way.

AS FOR ME, I breakfasted with Wolf and Ann-Marie for several hours over coffee and a delicious omelet seasoned with spices grown in their yard. Wolf is a retired professor of political science in this town of two colleges. Marie was a professor of German. Wolf has written a weekly column for the Jacksonville Journal-Courier for 23 years, more than twice as long as my 12-year run writing an online weekly column--so I consider him a veteran master of the craft. Following this multi-hour stimulating breakfast I headed to the Jacksonville library where the archivist helped me with accessing the county's resources on the Trail of Death, then graciously permitted me to write these drafts of my diary. I headed toward Exeter near lunchtime assuming I would not make it all the way. I simply drifted westerly and before long was in the town by accident, not due to purpose as much as my sloth in selecting a campsite for the night.

I have crossed the point in this trek where psychologically it is as if I am floating in a westward flowing river—my only job is to pick up each foot and let them float forward "with the current" toward the setting sun. This is how I found myself in Exeter just before dusk. However, my autopilot indolence paid off. Here in this town of 75 people I stayed with Paul Herring who with his wife Kate restored an old three-story hotel/school into a comfortable house that was built in 1860 on word that the railroad route would come through Exeter. The railroad never came. It went three miles to the north.

The original builder finally sold his hotel and it became a school for 75 years, and then fell into total disrepair. Paul and Kate bought the remains for $500 in 1973 and took the next few decades to restore it into a beautiful home. Paul is a math teacher in Jacksonville and Kate, once an attorney, now works for the Girl Scouts in Quincy and is in process of credentialing for ministry among the United Methodists. I showed up at his house while Paul still had some supper left in the large iron skillet, so once again the kindness of a Jacksonville-related person brought to me a wonderful meal and I was asleep by 9 p.m. having walked 16 miles this afternoon.

I'VE BEEN THINKING tonight about picking the wrong side. I don't know if there is such a thing as "bad luck" in war but if there is, the Indians seemed to have it. They kept siding with the white losers. The trouble with this was the generally-accepted principle (in both Europe and America) was the victors get land and losers lose it. This repeatedly hurt the Indians. The first great rivalry was between the French and the English. The Indians tended to side with the French. The French lost… and the Indians lost with them. In 1812 when the English fought the Americans, many Indians tended to side with the English. The English lost again, and so did the Indians. These alliances made it easier for white folk to demonize the Indians. More than 100 years later our government would herd into camps American citizens of Japanese ancestry because we were at war with Japan. In war it is easy to demonize the enemy (and anyone of the enemy's race) and to justify taking their land. I'm wondering tonight what might have happened if the Indians had sided with the winners in each case? Maybe nothing different.

Day 30-31 Naples, Illinois Mile 336
Oct. 3 & 4, 1838

In three hours the Potawatomi walked the nine miles from Exeter to the Illinois River at Naples, Illinois. This was the first mighty river of their journey. Naples was a primary port city on this river so it offered both keelboats and flatboats to ferry the Indians and wagons to the west shore. They spent the entire day crossing and re-crossing the river so that by 9 p.m. they had landed the final baggage wagon and camped on the shore opposite Naples. On their arrival at the river a child had died.

William Polke, the federal conductor of the expedition decided to take the next day off. Crossing the river had been exhausting work and the Potawatomi had been traveling every day now for a long time. Everyone needed a break so they took a zero mileage day to rest and catch up on the little duties that had been ignored too long. The Indians had been successfully hunting deer for more than a week so they now had plenty of deer hides with which to make new moccasins. Certainly they had previously made moccasins since it is unlikely that a single pair of moccasins could have lasted all 336 miles to the Illinois River. The Lewis and Clark expedition had made them every few days on the roughest part of their journey. Perhaps they even made some to put in stock for later use. The blankets and clothing needed washed. The journal was optimistic: *"the health of the Indians is now almost as good as before we commenced our march from Twin Lakes—a few days more will entirely recruit them."* The sick and weak—mostly children had died off including one child the day before. Immediately following this optimistic report the journal closes with *"A young child died this evening."* Apparently all the Indians were not in such good health. Soon there would be few children left.

FATHER PETIT had been sick with an attack of the fever for several days when they marched into Naples. He had refused the hospitality of the old Frenchman several days before, fearing he would get behind the Indians and again have a hard time catching up. Here in Naples a Protestant man (M. Craft) who had married a French Catholic woman from Vincennes heard there was a sick priest in the emigrating party and went to Petit and offered his house. Care was lavished on Petit and his fever broke. To finish up his cure he found yet another solution. Rather than staying back to recover he would jump ahead: *I took the public stage at Naples and started in advance for Quincy in order to complete my cure by a few days' rest."* By leap-frogging ahead of the emigrating party he arrived in Quincy several days before the Indians. Here he stayed with a German priest, Augustus

Brickwedde, who had been sent to Quincy to establish a German Catholic church a few years before. It would take the Indians several days to arrive at Quincy, and since the officers intended to stay at Quincy several more days, his leapfrogging enabled Petit to have an extended time for recuperation and recovery from his most recent bout with "the fever."

AS FOR ME I left the delightful night's rest at the Herrings and walked the quick four miles to Bluff, Illinois and picked up my mail. I had used Exeter as a mail drop, but discovered no post office in the tiny town. The "big" town in this region is Bluff (population 749). When the Post Office opened at nine I was there to collect several letters from friends and readers of my blog—THANKS! In the little park across the street I answered each letter and mailed them before stopping off at the one-room library in Bluff and chatting with the librarian about the region, then she let me use the library's "dial-up connection" to catch up posting my progress online.

I next walked into Naples in two more hours. Seven cars stopped on this short trip asking if I wanted a ride—usually only one or two a day do this. The difference? Huge dark thunderclouds with slicing lighting were rolling in from the west. I wonder if people have a natural inclination to "race for cover" in the presence of a severe thunderstorm and thus are quicker to offer to help you find cover as well? I do know that almost nobody ever offers a ride *during* a rainstorm, yet they all want to help as it threatens. It's interesting--what is this about people? It could be that knowing that this road dead ends in Naples makes people more comfortable picking up strangers? Anyway, I declined, but thanked each of them. I arrived in Naples just as the storm broke loose with a torrential downpour. I took cover in one of those little roadside wait-for-the-school-bus sheds for the next hour's drenching.

While sitting cozily in the lean-to matching golf carts purred up, driven by two gigantic men with matching beards and bellies—"We're brothers and kind of the sheriffs around here" they told me. "You that guy walking the long Indian walk?" I said I was. "Jerry told us about you--he had surgery and is recovering--but Bud here could take you across the river if Jerry doesn't." I was unable to rouse Jerry from his afterglow sleep so I left a note for him tucked in his door. Finding a person in a town of 137 people is not hard. Bud was a twenty-something local guy living in a trailer next to his dad. "It's my house and I own this land," he said. I helped Bud clean out his fishing boat on the trailer then Bud's mother showed up insisting, "You're not going out on that water—there's golf ball size hail coming." Indeed, another great dark thunder front was moving in so we waited for it to blow off a few dozen branches. Then, as soon as it passed, we launched and he dumped me on the western side of the river saying "Just walk through those woods until you find the power line then follow it to a road." He was right—I pushed through the woods and found the levee, then a gravel road and finally a paved road—though all the names of the road were different from my maps (why do counties rename their roads?). Here on this side of the river, the Potawatomi camped for two days. I would move on toward McKee's creek 12 miles on.

I'VE BEEN THINKING about watchers. I wonder how many residents stood on their porches in Naples and elsewhere *watching* the Potawatomi go by. I suspect many had compassion but just watched. I know some felt this was a terrible injustice—they said so to the Indians and others wrote about it. But still they stood by and watched. By this time there was nothing they could do about it, I guess, so they watched. Sometimes I watch too, because the time is past when an injustice can be avoided. What would I have done if I were working in my garden and saw this miles-long column of Indians moving westward on the road in front of my home? What injustices do I stand by and grieve about, but just *watch*?

Illinois River

Day 32 McKee's Creek (Perry, Illinois)—Mile 348
Oct. 5, 1838

The entry for October 5 is short. It only says, *"Left encampment opposite Naples at 8 o'clock and reached at a little after 12 our present encampment, at McKee's creek, twelve miles from the Illinois River. We were forced today to leave the road and travel a considerable distance to find water—even such as it is—standing in ponds—the streams are nearly all dry. Subsistence, beef and flour. Forage of a good character."*

That's it. Nothing more--just the location of the campsite, assessment of forage and food, and the perennial complaint about water. On any long trek there are many days that have no standout event. At least there were no deaths on this day. Sometimes nothing eventful is good news.

FATHER PETIT was in Quincy today, ahead of the rest of the emigrants by several days. The German priest there welcomed him happily as did four other families Petit listed in his diary. Apparently he recovered from his fever enough to eat dinner in the home of Richard Young, an Illinois representative to the U.S. Senate at the time.

AS FOR ME, once I left the river I walked on what the locals call "John Deere road" with only four vehicles passing me all afternoon. The fourth was an Schwan's Ice Cream truck and, half-in-jest I flagged it down with an ice-cream-cone-licking pantomime. Glancing over my shoulder I saw the truck's brake lights go on, then turn around in a lane down the road and come back to open up the store for me. I purchased a pint of raspberry-chocolate ice cream and ate all 1100 calories while walking toward the setting sun.

In Perry I found Darin and Nikki Mountain who have been faithfully following my journey on my blog and had written to me at every mail drop. Darin's great-great grandmother was Potawatomi but kept it quiet until the family unearthed the evidence in pictures and family memorabilia discovered years later. Darin makes gigantic radio transmitters sold mostly overseas and Nikki is a junior high school teacher who possesses the energy you'd expect from someone who is successful at that task. The Mountains gathered together a delightful collection of folk all involved in setting the Potawatomi monument here in Perry and we had a sweet evening of discussion. A reporter for the local newspaper, a retired school teacher, joined in and took notes as we talked. I spent the night in the Mountain's pop-up camper, which avoided me having to sleep in the rain and packing up a soaked tent the next morning. A huge thundershower came in the night.

I'VE BEEN THINKING all day about what to call "Native Americans." In 1838 it was not considered offensive to call them "savages" or "children" but proper terminology changes over the years. Negroes became colored people then became blacks and later became Afro-Americans and now (if I have this right) are African-Americans. What was once an acceptable label can later become offensive. Many Native Americans prefer to be called just that, "Native Americans." But not all. Some are quite satisfied with the misnomer "Indians" while others reject it completely. Many prefer only their tribal label: Potawatomi, Cherokee, Miami, and Navajo. I'm never sure when writing or speaking which to use so I tend to switch off from one to another (which only means some are miffed all of the time). In general I follow the advice, "Just ask" on these matters. Few races are offended when asked. I have the same problem with labeling the rest of us. Do I call us Anglos? Europeans? Whites? In the ideal world we would not have to use such labels I suppose. Then this book would about a group of *humans* who were removed to Kansas and all of us could be the descendants of both the perpetrators and the victims alike. Then we would all be both blamed and victimized by injustice. Would that be better or worse?

The Mountain family in Perry ,Illinois

Day 33 Hobson's Choice (Liberty, Illinois) Mile 366
Oct. 6, 1838

Dust was a constant trial for the Potawatomi. The drought had left the land powder dry and by the time almost a thousand people and more than 300 horses passed down a road, there would have been several inches of dust on the road like talcum powder billowing up and choking the riders and walkers. In a letter to his Bishop, Father Petit had described catching up to his congregation thus in Danville thus: *"Soon afterward I saw my poor Christians under a burning noonday sun, amidst clouds of dust, marching in a line, surrounded by militia who were hurrying their steps."* The billowing dust continued and must have blurred the eyes of both Indians and the militia and brought on hacking coughs.

On this day they got wonderful relief—RAIN! The journal puts it, *"During the night we were visited by a fall rain which rendered the traveling to-day unusually pleasant. The dust has been completely allayed, and the air much cooled."* After seven hours of travel over the rolling prairies, they pitched camp at a site they labeled "Hobson's Choice" near present-day Liberty, Illinois. "Hobson's choice" was an idiom of the day based on a story or fable of a man named Thomas Hobson who owned a livery in Cambridge, England, in the late 1500's and early 1600's. When a customer wanted a horse he supposedly told them to take the horse nearest the door or none at all—"Hobson's choice." It was the rough equivalent of our phrase today, "take it or leave it." The site was roundly condemned in the journal *"from the barrenness of the spot in everything save grass, brush and weeds, we have appropriately named Hobson's Choice."* By now the Potawatomi were used to ending the day as this one ended: *"A child died since we came into camp."* Somewhere near Liberty this child lies buried. I wonder where?

AS FOR ME I walked this day blessed repeatedly by the Mountain family—brothers, uncles, wives, husbands took it on themselves to meet me every hour or two on the road with ice water, bananas, apples, oranges, beef jerky and nuts so that on this day I probably actually gained weight! Interesting turnaround: when the Potawatomi passed through Jacksonville just a few days ago the whites blessed them with gifts. Now more than 150 years later Potawatomi descendants bless a white man on the road with gifts.

I'VE BEEN THINKING about being needy. I've already thought about how I can see God's image in the character of the many people who offer help to me—kindness, compassion, and generosity. Tonight I'm wondering why I don't notice that so clearly in ordinary life. Don't the people I work with and students I teach have as much generosity as these strangers I meet on the road? Why am I seeing such kindness and generosity out here that seems far more than I ever see normally? I thought of an answer to that question while walking today. I think it is because I'm so *needy* out here. People offer me rides because I am walking along a lonely country road. They offer me spare bedrooms because the alternative is sleeping on the ground. They offer me cold drinks because streams of sweat are pouring down my face and the sun is burning my skin. They feed me because I am not in a Winnebago camper but walking with a tiny pack on my back without food. In short, I'm needy. Maybe I need to be more *needy* in ordinary life?

Day 34 Mill Creek (near Quincy, Illinois) Mile 378
Oct. 7, 1838

Polke generally camped outside of a large city or on the opposite shore of a river town, probably to avoid any trouble in town and to especially deprive the militia, wagoners and Indians of alcohol, which often led to trouble between an organized traveling party and a town. In the case of Quincy he did both -- stopping short of town at Mill Creek, then crossing the Mississippi river and staying several days on the western shore.

The twelve mile trip from Hobson's Choice campsite to Mill Creek passed over rolling hills then across a high level prairie before dropping slightly to Mill creek. Polke planned to get up early in the morning and get the entire party safely across the river, then take several days *"to allow the teamsters and others engaged in the service, sufficient time to repair their wagons, etc."*

Other than reporting the journey pleasant and *"better than usual supplied with water"* the only other item is the almost daily common line closing out the journal, *"a child died shortly after we arrived in camp."*

AS FOR ME, after visiting the marker in Liberty, I walked to Mill Creek with little news and little thought. At the Mill Creek historical marker I sat soaked in the humidity until Sharon arrived the now—410 mile distance from our home in Marion, Indiana. The party of Indians took several days off on the western shore of the Mississippi and so shall I.

The halfway mark should be a celebration for me but it's not. It seems like this journey should be over by now, not merely half-over. I am tired and worn-out, have blisters on my feet and the bones in my ankles, heels and knees are screaming, "Go home with your wife tomorrow!" I am tired of walking, tired of eating whatever I can find, and tired of sleeping on the ground. I'm tired of the sun, tired of noisy trucks and dirty roads and the overly humid heat. I am tired of writing blog entries that I'm not sure are being read, tired of thinking about Indians 150 years ago constantly, and tired of this whole business. I'm *tired*.

I want to switch channels. I want to think of something else. Go home and write great prose in my air-conditioned writer's studio. Attend a good movie. Read a book I don't have to carry in my pack. Sleep in my own bed. Go out to a quiet dinner with our friends. I'm tired of this trek. The romance and adventure have been replaced by drudgery. I want to quit. This is how I'm feeling here at the Mill Creek marker, waiting for Sharon to arrive. Maybe I'll quit.

I'VE BEEN THINKING about social Darwinism. A surprising number of Christians actually ascribe to this theory. The idea is that there will always be an underclass so life is based on the "survival of the fittest" who can scramble up out of poverty. Those who espouse this idea say, "the poor you have with you always" and assume that inequities are not a result of injustice or unfair distribution but the result of the laziness and lethargy of the poor. They assume that if the underclass would simply work as hard as ordinary people do they would be able to "pull themselves up by their own bootstraps." Social Darwinists approach Native American history by saying that the death of the stone age hunter-gatherer culture was inevitable and only Indians who adapted could survive, the rest who clung to antique appendages or old culture must eventually pass away, or at least remain a permanent underclass. Indians schools where children were punished for saying an Indian word were considered an "enlightened" attempt to force the Indians to adapt to survive. While the attempts are more sophisticated today, the issue remains. The trouble with Social Darwinism for a Christian is that the stronger culture is not always the better one.

Mill Creek: It is hot and humid and seems like time to give up and go home

Day 35-37 Quincy, Illinois—Mile 384
Oct. 8-10, 1838

This was an entire village moving to Kansas—young people, newborn babies, pregnant women, middle aged men with bad knees, and grandparents who could barely walk. It would be like going down the street to select randomly 900 people from your neighborhood, announcing they must begin a walk to Kansas. And they had white militia guarding them, plus wagon-drivers on contract with the government. All this mixed group of people had more to do than travel. There were moccasins to make, clothes to wash, wagon spokes to repair and salaries to the contract workers to be paid. The party did this on the west shore of the Mississippi facing Quincy.

When the Indians passed through Quincy, they attended the St. Boniface church--a brand new congregation of German Catholics, according to the congregation's own history. In that book, which local archeologist, Steve Tieken loaned to me, it claims that Quincy was at the time perhaps 300 people, with 250 of them being German Catholics. This sounds small to me, but so far it is all I have to go on. According to that church record their little frame church had been built just that year. This is the only constructed church the Catholic Indians worshipped in since they had left behind in Twin Lakes their beloved log chapel they had built with their own hands.

Accounts were organized and the officers, laborers and wagoners were paid. Two militiamen and a wagoner decided they'd had enough and requested discharge to go home—and they were discharged. Several of the chiefs met with Polke asking that they not travel any more on the "Sabbath" so they could hold "devotional exercises." Our intermittent Doctor Jerolaman returned to the migrating party here in Quincy, having joined the group late, then gotten sick September 24, left the group in Springfield the 29th and now returned to work October 9th—having missed about 25% of the trip in this instance alone—I will be interested to see if he is "docked" for this when he is paid at the end of the trip (the payment records still exist).

These days were given to organizing, paying, sorting, packing and repacking the wagons along with shoeing the horses and repairing the wagons for the second half of the trip. All this required them to ferry back and forth into town for supplies since they were camping on the opposite shore from town. The official journal spins the frequent shuttles this way: *"This might have been avoided by remaining on the Quincy shore, but the dissolute habits of the Indians and their great proneness to intoxication, forbid such a step..."* This seems to be a change of tone in the journal from previous entries where the writer seems to brag about "nothing of the sort" of drunkenness being allowed. And it was particularly hard on the Indians, some of which were Menominee's Catholics committed to total abstinence anyway. What had changed? I don't know. By evening of October 10th they were ready to push on for the second leg of their journey.

FATHER PETIT probably continued staying with the German priest, Augustus Brickwedde, while in Quincy as he continued to recover from the fever. The Catholic hospitality to this traveling priest gives us a glimpse of the minority status of Catholics (also Frenchmen, and Germans) in the USA at that time. The dominant religious persuasion of America was Christian-Protestant. Catholics were a minority group. Thus the Catholic Potawatomi who were a racial minority also were in the religious minority. However, as with all minority groups, there is kind hospitality extended to others in the group. Quincy was an exception in America (assuming the church's history book is correct in suggesting the town had a *majority* of German Catholic population) but Petit could expect Catholics everywhere to extend hospitality as he traveled.

Minority religious groups often feel compelled to prove their superiority –especially among themselves. This may have been the root cause of Petit's reporting of an incident that happened while he was in Quincy, when a Catholic woman and her Protestant friend came out to see the Indians. Here it is in Petit's own words: *"A Catholic lady, accompanied by a Protestant friend, made the sign of the cross, symbolizing religious fraternity. Immediately the Indian women came up to shake hands cordially; the savages never fail to do this when they encounter Catholics. The Protestant lady wanted to do as much and tried the sign of the cross, but betrayed by her lack of practice, she could not succeed. At once the Indians, who knew some English, went up to her and said, 'You nothing.' It was true."*

Today we might consider his attitude repugnant. However in that day religious people, even Baptists and Methodists had similar attitudes toward each other, though both were Protestants. And we shall soon see that attitudes toward the Mormons was even more severe. Most Christians today have far greater tolerance of those in other denominations and would never approve of a blunt pronouncement "You nothing" just because they are not in the "right" denomination. However, at the same time there are still such attitudes under the surface. In our American free enterprise culture, denominations seem to be inclined to advertise themselves as the only true church and label all other denominations as ineffective ways to heaven. Petit's report to his Bishop of this event detracts from his reputation if we judge him by from today's more tolerant approach. However at that time we can at least remember Catholics were a tiny minority, they were considered a totally false religion by most Protestants, and he was writing to his Bishop in reporting this event. The incident is a useful example to us of the free market competition among American Christian denominations in 1838.

There were white-trash hangers-on following the emigration for personal profit. In a letter from Polke to Carey Harris, Commissioner of Indian Affairs in Washington D.C. which was sent from Quincy Polke describes keeping fifteen "militia" for two purposes: The second reason was to guard the "grogshops" "with which each village abounds" but the first is more revealing. He kept the militia to control the *"suspicious persons who"* [next line crossed out in his rough draft of the letter but not in the final draft sent] *"who are following the emigration with a view as is supposed"* [then the final draft says in its place, *"frequent our camps with a view of swindling the Indians of their ponies and other property..."*

Petit stocked up on supplies in Quincy. The town's location on the river enabled it to have supplies far greater than a small village would normally have had available. Petit recorded every cent he spent or lent in his journal. His expenditures give us a glimpse of the sort of things he bought. He had spent $4.50 to ride the stage from Naples to Quincy. At Quincy he spent $15.00 on supplies including *"boots, blankets, hose, wine, raisins, goggles, books, &c."* When Petit left Quincy, Father Brickwedde presented him with a pipe as a gift, which he also listed in his daily pastor's journal.

AS FOR ME I also took several days off in Quincy with Sharon. We both had a delightful supper with Steve and Janet Tieken. Steve is an Archeologist and plans to walk with me on Monday through Quincy. I also got to interview the priest at St. Boniface church and attend a service there. The rest of the weekend was spent sleeping and giving myself to purposeful laziness in order to charge my batteries physically for the walk across Missouri, which Shirley Willard warns me, will be like walking through a 90-degree steam room. I leave Monday morning to walk with Steve Tieken. On Tuesday Ryan Robertson, a recent Indiana Wesleyan University graduate headed into teaching will join me for the day. After that I'm on my own in the steam room.

I'VE BEEN THINKING about denominational competition. We've come a long ways since 1838, and few today would say, "You nothing" to someone of another denomination. Yet some Christians (some entire denominations) still harbor that attitude even though they refrain from saying the actual words. It is often what we *don't* say that bequeaths this attitude to our children. This is not to say Catholics and Protestants are "all saying the same thing." There are differences, but on the core issues of Christian faith—the elements of the Apostle's Creed—we stand firm and in full agreement. I wonder how people a hundred years from now will look at my attitude toward others. Will they be mortified by the way I treat someone and will they be embarrassed for me like I am embarrassed by Father Petit's response?

Mark Schmerse and his wife Jessica join the walk for a day

Don Gander, Ryan Robertson, Josephine Gander, & Keith Drury

Day 38 Pleasant Spring (Palmyra, Missouri)—Mile 387
Oct. 11, 1838

The longer rest at Quincy must have restored the Indians' spirits and bodies. The journal puts it, *"The rest of yesterday and the day before had much recruited the health and spirits of the Indians."* The day's march was *"without the occurrence of any difficulties."* At Pleasant Spring (near present Palmyra) Capt. J. Holman arrived to become an Assistant Superintendent of the government-sponsored removal. Why he shows up at this point in the journey and what secret political machinations were going on behind the scene are not told. Only that he had "*received his appointment at the suggestion of reports unfavorable to the health of the officers.*" What were these reports? What was wrong with the health of the officers that Dr. Jerolaman had not cared for? Was this medical or otherwise? Who knows? All we know is Capt. Holman shows up as a new Assistant Superintendent.

One of the wagons had lost its oxen and had to stay behind at the Mississippi until it rounded up the escaped beasts. The rest of the group traveled over the flat flood plain of the Mississippi to Pleasant Spring—nicely named, though it was not pleasant for all. An adult woman died shortly after they made camp.

FATHER PETIT recorded in his diary today, *"the health at camp improves."* It must have been a great relief for him to see the reduced number of deaths after Quincy. This is a two-bladed sword: while there were fewer deaths, there were simply fewer children and aged left to die. The string of regular deaths across Indiana and Illinois must have haunted everyone, bringing a tearless pall over the Indians who left so many of their children along the way. But the Indians were refreshed now and they were hoping for cooler weather and maybe even some rain so they could escape the swirling dust of the roads. They were about to get more than they hoped for.

AS FOR ME my days off at Quincy restored me as it had the Indians. I started at Mill Creek where I had ended the week before in total mental and physical exhaustion and walked to the river with archeologist Steve Tieken and that gave me a chance to hear the awesome story of his own spiritual journey. After an interview with WGEM TV (which was broadcast that night) Steve's wife Janet took me across the Mississippi bridge which allowed no foot travel. On the western shore I headed out only to be found by Mark and Jessica Schmerse former students of mine from the quad cities who had driven down to "walk a day with coach D." We walked in burning sun all day but the delightful conversation was by all means worth it. In the late afternoon while sitting in the heat beside a side road I had another "Schwan's experience." This time a Schwan's ice cream truck pulled off without invitation and out popped the woman driver who opened a side door and brought us three ice cream cones and said, "I saw you way back at Quincy and now you're here—this is for you." Before this trip I hardly knew of these deliver-to-your-home ice cream people—but I know about them now!

With threatening thunderstorms rolling in I left Mark and Jess hitching back to their car and made my camp under a power line above Palmyra and went asleep just before a gentle rain began to fall. An hour or two later I woke up to a light in the front of my tent door—it was Ryan Robertson, a recent Indiana Wesleyan University graduate now seeking a job as a teacher. He had found out the general location of my campsite from Mark and Jess, announcing he planned to walk with me the next day and wanted to come at night "to get a full 24 hour experience." I made room in my tent and soon we were both asleep preparing for the next day's travel.

I'VE BEEN THINKING today about *systems*. The removal was a terrible injustice done to the Potawatomi but it is hard to pin the evil on any one person. The wrong was a wrongful system—"systemic injustice." The *government* was in on it—as it responded to overwhelming public opinion of the *voters*. Indeed, when the *Supreme Court* decided an important case in favor of the Cherokee, but President Andrew Jackson, reportedly said, "[Chief Justice] John Marshall has made his decision; let him enforce it now if he can." The courts had no soldiers, so popular opinion won. And the Indians lost. The *Indiana State government* was part of the system too: they bought cheap Indian land then sold it to new taxpayers at a markup and built canals, bridges and roads with the profit. The *settlers* were hungry for new land. The *traders* played a major role in the whole fiasco by selling supplies to the unsuspecting Indians at up to ten times more than the town prices and selling on credit—"just place your "X" here and take it with you." They then piled up these debts against the next annuity payments or next land sale income. One can readily see how easy it would be to juggle the books, add to the list and mark your own "X" in the space behind these additional entries. This is why the "sale" money usually never got to the Indians—it went straight to the traders to pay off the mountainous debt they had accumulated since the last sale. And even the Indian *chiefs* were sometimes in on it too. Some unscrupulous chiefs took massive pay-offs personally and failed to pass on the money to their own followers or tribe. The loser in all this was, as always, the common Indian…and all of us.

Day 39 See's Creek, Missouri—Mile 410
Oct. 12, 1838

The Potawatomi now were traversing rolling hills and having camped outside of town they passed through Palmyra at ten in the morning. It must have been quite a spectacle for these small towns to see 700-800 Indians and their guards pass through town single file—a column almost three miles in length. One risk was that the Indians (or the militia) would buy liquor in these towns, get drunk and cause trouble with the townsfolk who may have been delighted to respond. Everyone was watched carefully, but it is difficult to keep a motivated buyer from meeting a motivated seller and the journal reports, *"two or three Indians were found to have procured liquor and became much intoxicated."* They were arrested and put under guard until they slept it off.

The health of the Indians was improving because *"medicine has not been for some time administered to them."* They reported the wagoner who had lost his oxen had caught up to the column and in a simple line that must hide tremendous maneuvering the journal says, *"Gen. A. Morgan, who has heretofore been acting in the capacity of Assistant Superintendent in the emigration gave notice that he should offer his resignation to-morrow."* The day before, Capt. Holman had arrived as an Assistant Superintendent and today Morgan announces his resignation.

What was going on? We do know that General Tipton thought very little of Morgan. He had written September 3 to Abel Pepper, *"Gen'l Morgan hangs on to the emigration although we were compelled to stop him from even dividing the provisions to the Indians for which he is wholly unfit, without personal respect or sense of honor he will cling to the noxious vapors of an Indian camp for money the sport of every wag."* What did this mean? Was Morgan crooked and used the Indians as a means of profit? Or did he identify with the Indians and hung around their camp instead of staying with the elite fellow officers, some of whom even had their own personal servants along to cook for them?

I have seen this among missionaries—the missionary who identifies too much with the people (instead of their fellow missionaries) almost always is rejected by other missionaries. Was this the case for Gen'l Morgan? Is he a good guy in this story who was identifying with the Indians instead of the white militia or was he out to make money off the Indians? Father Petit had stayed with Morgan in his tent when he caught up with the emigration. Did this mean anything? Morgan did make some money on this trip. He was paid

$594 for his work—only the federal conductor, Polke ($842) and Doctor Jerolaman ($908) received more money in the list of final accounting. Was he an incompetent officer hanging on just for this pay? Was he making money off the distribution of the provisions or selling to the Indians? Was he promising things to the Indians beyond the treaty? For instance, was Morgan also giving the Indians the idea there would be houses for them in Kansas? None of the treaties say such a thing in print. We just don't know. All we know is one day Capt. Holman shows up and the very next day General Morgan announces he will resign the following day. And why announce it ahead of time—"I plan to resign tomorrow?" Why not just resign today? What was really going on here?

AS FOR ME, Ryan and I picked up a big breakfast at the Hardies where one of the Trail of Death markers is located and walked all day on gravel roads in the blistering sun. In a late afternoon, while I was sprawled out in the tall grasses picking ticks off our legs, Don and Liz Gander appeared in their car with cookies and a cooler of iced drinks. They announced I would stay tonight with Josephine Gander, an 89-year-old woman who has sponsored two of the trail markers and still lives in the farmhouse she moved into the year I was born (1945). She had been married in 1937 but moved into this house in 1945. The house itself was built in 1918. Picking up the pace, we walked to Mt Vernon church where the marker is located remembering the See's Creek campsite, where three women were baking cinnamon rolls for the church's bake sale and insisted we have one each to encourage us on our way. Ryan had planned to hitch back to his car in Palmyra but Liz insisted she would take him back after dinner. 89 years old yet spry and with an exceedingly sharp mind, Josephine Gander prepared a meal of garden corn, beans, creamed potatoes, and ham and topped it off with pineapple-coconut pie before Liz took Ryan back to his car and I retired for the night before dark in this old farm house built before I was born.

I'VE BEEN THINKING this evening about "Missiology." Early missionaries were sometimes an agent of culture and nationalism as much as agents of Christ. Today's missionaries are carefully trained as professionals in "missiology" or the science of intercultural ministry. At the core of this approach is the pealing away from religious practice those things that are cultural and national until only the universal trans-cultural core remains. Once this pealing away is done there is precious little remaining of our traditional ways of doing religion. It is both little and it is precious.

Day 40 Clinton (North Fork, Missouri) – Mile 427
Oct. 13-14 1838

The political intrigue thickened on this day as General Morgan prepared to leave. Chief Ash-kem and others came to the headquarters first thing in the morning before departing to Clinton, to speak with Polke, the federal conductor of the outfit. They stated they were not happy with Morgan's leaving. There were promises Morgan had made they were not sure would be kept in his absence. They also requested that they travel less and remain in camp longer. Here is one hint that General Morgan had made some promises representing the government. Though I have suspected Tipton made the most explicit promises (after all, he was in a place where he could keep the promises—in the U. S. Senate), apparently Morgan made similar promises. I don't know what I think of Morgan yet.

However the Indians were not unanimous in their support of Morgan. While Ash-kum and his group rejected Morgan's leaving, Chief I-o-weh disagreed "*in strong terms*" stating that these other men were not in fact chiefs at all and were thus not entitled respect as such.

It was often true in the white's negotiations with the Indians (and usually to the disadvantage of the Indians), the competing tribes and competing chiefs undercut each other and allowed the whites to almost always find at least one "chief" on their side so that they could claim they had agreement from the Indians. Indeed the whole land "purchase" was accomplished without all the chiefs signing—and some chiefs (and especially the whites) claimed that certain men were not chiefs at all (e.g. Tipton's claim that Menominee was not a chief). Where the Indians were divided, they almost always lost. And they were often divided.

We do not know what really happened behind the scenes. Polke stated that General Morgan had offered his resignation *voluntarily,* and then Morgan himself thanked the Indians for their support and promptly left before the emigration moved on for Clinton. As they traveled to Clinton, Missouri (present day, North Fork) the day was windy and dusty and "*exceedingly afflicting.*" They arrived at Clinton by 3 p.m. and camped after a hard day facing wind and dust.

As to their request to travel fewer daily miles, it is not clear it was seriously considered. So far they had walked 427 miles in 40 days--less than 10 miles per day average. In the next dozen days they would walk another

119 miles with three days off, an average of about ten miles a day--13 miles a day figuring walking days. Was Polke like many of today's leaders who listen intently to complaints of their people then simply ignore them? Some leaders even admit this is their strategy: "Just listen to complaints—all they really want is to be heard." However, it may have *seemed* to have an effect—since the group was now taking every Sunday off, which may have felt like lowering the miles. Actually getting to Kansas before the bitter cold of winter was in the best interest of all. And, the white militiamen were likely wanting to get home before Christmas.

AS FOR ME I left with several of Josephine's sausage biscuits in my pack and decided to take a few shorter days as blister treatment—several the size of silver dollars are nagging me on both heals. Walking on gravel roads also supplied some foot relief. I stopped for water at a nearby farmhouse to be greeted by Shane McClintic, "Sure—I saw you on TV" (Quincy's WGEM news coverage). Not only did I get cold water, Shane constructed a giant sandwich of homemade bread piled with slabs of ham and cheese. I sometimes feel guilty for taking all this generosity considering the original travelers' pain. I wonder how an Indian would be treated today taking this walk. Any differently? I camped for the night by mid afternoon as a great rainstorm rolled in I planned to sleep late the next day--say, 7 a.m. or so.

I'VE BEEN THINKING about evil. The removal of these Indians by Whites was an evil deed. White people bear the burden for this. But evil knows no racial boundaries. Condemning the evil of the whites is not to say Indians are born without evil. Indian tribes were killing and making slaves of each other before Europeans arrived. Inter-tribal racism existed before whites expressed their own anti-Indian racism. Evil does not reside in one race and not the others. Evil lies in the heart of all human beings. Yet the evil of the whites seems worse. Why? Is it because the Europeans were so *entrepreneurial*? Indians scalped other tribes before whites arrived, but the sophisticated Europeans introduced the idea of *buying* those scalps. French and English powers bought white scalps like they bought beaver pelts. This seems a worse kind of evil to me. And, while Indians visited evil on other tribes with their tomahawks, the shear industrial might of the European's canons and guns made war so much worse. Sure, evil lies in the heart of all humans. But *sophisticated mechanized entrepreneurial evil* seems worse. Yet it is true that neither white nor red man can be blamed for evil. The battle line between good and evil is not drawn between Tipton and Petit, white and red, one nation or another. The line between good and evil runs through the heart of every human being.

Day 41 Clinton, Missouri—Mile 427
Oct. 14, 1838

The Indians had been promised in Quincy they'd get Sundays off for worship and Polke kept his promise. They stayed a second day in Clinton. Father Petit gathered his flock for an extended worship service—much longer than the usual morning and evening prayers.

On Sunday evening the political intrigue returned. General Morgan was gone. That was a lost cause now. The next issue related to Doctor Jerolaman. Chief Ash-Kum and I-o-weh were in total agreement on this issue: get rid of Doctor Jerolaman. The journal says the two chiefs along with others came to *"demand the dismissal or suspension of Dr. Jerolaman, the physician for the emigration whom they had ceased to like and did not wish him longer to accompany the emigration."*

What had Jerolaman done? Was it a common ground unifying demand that both Ash-Kum and I-o-weh could now agree on? While they differed on Morgan, they agreed wholeheartedly on Jerolaman—he must go. Why? In a letter from Polke he had described the *"improper course"* taken by Dr. Jerolaman hinting at some impropriety. What was the course he had taken that was improper? An even more revealing hint is that the word "course" was a later substitution—the first word he used in his draft that was later crossed out said "Improper conduct." What had happened? What sort of "conduct" or "course" had the doctor taken that was improper? We are left to guess. Something so infuriated the Indians enough to demand his dismissal. Even Polke agreed that the Doctor's conduct (or course) was improper. Judge Polke determined to submit the whole case to the Department for them to decide. What happened to this charge—was it overlooked later? What had the doctor done? I don't know and can only guess.

Was it his bedside manner –did he despise the Indians and they caught his attitude? Was it his intermittent presence—especially in Indiana and Illinois when all their children had been dying—i.e. "Where were you when our babies were dying—you were in your comfortable town and now you show up when most of them are dead?" Did they sense the fat paycheck he would collect at the end of this expedition and compared that to his effort and presence? (As mentioned before, he would get in cash the equivalent of 908 acres of Indian land). That was a tidy sum for two months work where all expenses are paid and you get a generous sick day policy that enables you to stay in comfortable towns when the Indians need you most. What caused their insistence that the doctor be fired? Or was he guilty of some other improper behavior after hours or at night? Who knows?

Whatever, the Indians were dealing with a judge. Judge Polke was not given to rash decisions and answered the chiefs by informing them *"that their request was one of so much importance and so unusual in emigration, that he hoped he might be allowed time not only to decide himself but to council with his officers."* This seemed to satisfy the Indians with the promise that a final answer would be given the next evening.

AS FOR ME my regimen for healing the silver-dollar-blisters on my heels is to walk less, rest more and air out my feet every hour. That strategy failed today. It rained all night—six inches local farmers claimed. It was still raining the next morning when I took down my tent and packed up my now-soggy sleeping bag. I am thinking of the Potawatomi folding their wool blankets, chuckling that the dampness in their wool was far better than dampness in modern down sleeping bags. I walked my five miles into Clinton/North Fork by noon in pouring rain. There Don and Liz Gander met me again—the son and daughter-in-law of Josephine Gander with whom I had stayed two nights before. They had driven all the way from Monroe City to bring a Sub sandwich and some soda for my lunch. Joining them out of the rain in their pick-up truck I wolfed down the sandwich and chatted one final time before bidding this wonderful family goodbye. I now carry in my pocket an arrowhead found by Josephine's late husband who was a farmer and "could see an arrowhead from 25 feet while on a tractor." She had given it to me as I departed the day before. I carry it as precious cargo and must find some way to treat it with respect. Now I bid farewell to her son and his wife, Liz. I got a quick hug from Don, a retired Air Force officer who is probably not given to hugs, then headed south toward Paris in the pouring rain, secretly hoping I'd make it before dark. When it rains I always hope there will be a motel or guest room in some town ahead. I hate camping in the rain—especially when my sleeping bag is already soggy.

I'VE BEEN THINKING this afternoon about government contractors. I don't know what was going on with Dr. Jerolaman and I can't prove anything but I don't trust him. I have to admit I was a bit happy the Indians confirmed my suspicions. Maybe we are both wrong about him, but I don't like the fellow. I think he got paid way too much for doing way too little. But perhaps that is how we feel about a lot of government contractors. When the government gets ready to spend a lot of money "helping people," some of the contractors seem to get the most help.

Day 42 Paris, Missouri –Mile 439
Oct. 15, 1838

It took the group only four hours to cover the twelve miles from Clinton to Paris. A strong wind had come up *"which rendered our passage across the prairie very disagreeable. Many of the Indians suffered a good deal."* The writer of the journal didn't know it, but this wind may have been their first hint at what was to come next—a major shift in the weather and the kind of trials they would face traveling. The heat and dust would exchange places soon with cold and mud.

In the evening at Paris the chiefs assembled to receive the answer to their demands that Doctor Jerolaman be terminated. *"A large number of the Indians came up to Head Quarters and repeated their request of last night."* This time the speaker strengthened their demands, saying he *"did not demand it for himself or for his associates alone, but for every man, woman and child in the camp—they all united in soliciting [Polke] discharge Dr. Jerolaman."*

In response Judge Polke "divided the baby." He told the Indians they were free to refuse to be treated by Jerolaman but that he would be retained to treat the officers. This was how Polke wriggled the government out of a sticky situation. Then Polke pled with the Indians to not let this dispute mar the otherwise unity of the trip thus far or cause any dissention or bad feelings between *"the officers and their red brethren."* Then to conclude the negotiation successfully he announced he had bought a keg of tobacco, which he *"wished them to smoke in token of continued friendship."* Tobacco was the token of resolution. The Indians then retired but requested the opportunity to raise the Jerolaman issue again. The journal does not record the issue coming up again—the judgment of Polke (along with a keg of tobacco) apparently resolved the issue for the time being.

FATHER PETIT got invited to breakfast today. Word of a Catholic priest among the captive Indians must have gotten into town ahead of the group. Several Catholics came out to visit him and invited him to eat breakfast with them before leaving Paris. It was in Paris where an incident occurred with a Baptist minister. As it is written by Petit it sheds light on the denominational competition of the day so I include it here as he wrote it: *" ...Judge Polke, our principle officer, introduced one of his friends, a Baptist minister. I was in my tent, surrounded as usual by Indians. He wanted to shake hands with the Indians, and I told them to approach—that he called himself a friend. Then, as if he must make a sensation, this minister, with the commanding enthusiasm in which his kind are never lacking, cried: 'Ah, they* *are bone of my bone, flesh of my flesh! I truly feel here [putting his hand on his heart] that I love humankind. Young man, may God bless your labors among them—make them better than they are.' When he had gone, I told the Indians that he was a Protestant minister. At this all that who shaken hands with him replied with a grimace."*

This is a companion incident to the one in Quincy where the Protestant woman fumbled an attempt at making the sign of the cross and the Indian responded with, "You nothing." We must remember that Petit is writing to his Bishop who expects him to make inroads for Catholics among the Indians, so Petit may be showing himself to be more narrow-minded than he really was. He places the "You nothing" words in the Indian's mouths, and assigns the grimace here to the Indians not to himself. He may have been doing a bit of public relations, showing his Bishop the Catholic devotion of his parishioners and their resistance to evangelistic Protestants. We also recall that Menominee had a relationship with the Baptist mission in Ft. Wayne, and there were among the Indians some strong Baptists too— including Joseph Bourassa and others who had been schooled in the Baptist mission in Niles, Michigan, where Polke had taught for two years. (Indeed, Polke had married the sister of the founder of this mission). So there already was some low-level competition between the Baptists and Catholics among the Potawatomi. Petit may have been showing his Bishop that his flock was intensely loyal as Catholics and not likely to switch easily. But it is embarrassing to us today, a sort of "denominational racism."

Inter-Nicene competition was common among denominations at the time. Perhaps this sort of attitude was probably really Petit's attitude as well. Protestants and Catholics had been killing each other in Europe not too long before. They would continue doing so in Northern Ireland even in the late 20th century. While Christians today are more generous and ecumenical, there is even today plenty of interdenominational competition and rejection. I think Petit's report accurately reflects Petit's own views. He could work with Baptists but he was gratified when his congregation rejected them. The Baptists probably felt likewise about the Catholics—maybe more so.

However, the report does give us a glimpse into the two competing denominations. Catholics went about their mission more quietly than Baptists. Petit was put off by the noisy attempt to speechify and make a sensation. Yet the Baptist minister was likely expressing himself honestly and did indeed feel a kinship with the Indians. The minister even went so far as to bless Petit's (Catholic) work with them—no small olive branch from a Baptist in that day. Petit does not seem to return the favor by blessing the Baptist (though he may have done so personally and not reported it here to his Bishop). It is true that Protestants today are more likely to bless Catholic ministry than *vice versa*. Protestants are used to many denominations and many have come to consider Roman Catholics "another Christian denomination." This is harder for Catholics to do—having considered themselves so long as the one true church. However, a kinder more gentle spirit of ecumenical generosity has prevailed more recently as both Protestants and Catholics find themselves cooperating on moral and ethical issues. Whatever, these two stories from Petit's letter illustrate the roots of present-day competitive attitudes between Christian denominations.

AS FOR ME I continued on from my sub-sandwich lunch at Clinton in the pouring rain across swollen creeks and along tiny gravel roads. Having lost the sun I navigated by sense and headed south to Paris, secretly hoping I'd make it before dark to a motel. I noted that the wind had shifted directions and I took one turn, then another carefully keeping track of which way was south. After three or four hours of walking in soaking rain I finally came to a paved road. I was uncertain as to which way to turn—the first time I was not clear of directions on this trip. I knocked on a nearby farmhouse and a grizzled old man shuffled to the door to tell me I needed to turn back around and head back down the long road on which I had just arrived. Certainly he was wrong! I argued a bit with the fellow and pointed to my map but his eyes glinted as he said, "Sonny, I don't care what your map says, this is road CC and Paris is *that* way." Sure enough I had walked several hours and wound up north of where I had started hours before on my southward journey. The wind had not shifted—I had shifted. Returning down a long route you've already walked is the hardest walking one does—a "repentance" of sorts.

The rain did clear off by suppertime and I was making progress toward Paris. Passing one house, two women were inspecting their garden in the diminishing rain and I asked, "Is there a motel in Paris?" They shouted back—"three miles below town." Then they asked where I was walking. After hearing my answer they invited me to sit a spell on their patio for coffee and cookies, an invitation I gladly accepted. I pretended to myself that the day was just starting and this was my morning coffee—that seemed to improve my attitude.

After Lois' coffee I set out with renewed energy and determination to make it to Paris and that motel. On my cell phone I got a call from Nancy Stone, president of the Monroe County Historical Society, who promised me she'd take me out to the motel so I did not have to walk three miles off my route—six miles extra as a round trip. As soon as I got to the blinker light in Paris, she met me and after a meal of several hamburgers dropped me off at the motel where I adjusted the under-the-window heater to 95 degrees, which converted the entire motel room into a virtual drier. Spreading all my gear about the room I went to sleep in the drier. By morning everything was dry and plenty warm.

On Friday morning I stayed in Paris—where I was scheduled to arrive today. I had breakfast with Nancy Stone and the kindly restaurant owner picked up my ticket, refusing to let me pay a cent. "If you can walk here all the way from Indiana, you shouldn't have to buy your own breakfast!" What kindness I've experienced!

Then there's the Post Office story. I had listed Paris, Missouri, as a mail drop on my web site. Nancy Stone told me last night that there'd be trouble. "You listed the zip code for Paris, Illinois, not Paris, Missouri" she told me. *Oh Oh*! I went to the post office in the wrong state and offered my license, realizing that my mail was in the next state. "Oh, it's you!" the postmistress said. She told me how the postmaster in Paris, Illinois had called her to ask if she knew who Keith Drury was—she said no. Then the Illinois postmaster got some mail forwarded from Exeter/Bluff where I had passed through a week before. The postmaster called them and they said, "Oh yes—that's the guy walking the Trail of Death and he's headed west." They figured out that the trail went through Paris, Missouri, and thus forwarded a whole bundle of mail to the "wrong" state, which was actually the right state. The pile was waiting for me here! I love the postal employees in these little towns!

The whole affair reminded me of another incident. While hiking on the Pacific Crest Trail a few years ago, I apparently lost my credit card at one of my campsites. This is easy to do, since in the woods things like food, and water, and camping gear are vital and a credit card or money is totally useless and often left floating around in the pack until one gets to town. When I arrived at the next town I discovered my card (my credit card) was missing and called Sharon to have another sent to the next post office up the line—a week later. I continued on that hike for another six weeks before returning home to Marion, Indiana. The next October, months later, I received an envelope with the credit card and a little note saying, "Another hiker found this card in the mountains and turned it in to our post office and they asked us to find you." The story: the postmistress had figured out I was headed north and forwarded the card to the next post office I would "probably" be visiting, and from there it bounced to the next PO up the line until weeks later, it came to the final post office for that hike and they found my home address left for forwarding mail. This kind of care and service is from those "government employees" people often scorn today.

While sitting on the park bench reading my mail the librarian showed up and invited me in before the noon opening to use their computer. The rest of the afternoon I spent updating this journal. I was interrupted only for an interview by the local newspaper, and then some TV filming from a distant station (KTVO) where they plan to run a piece on the Trail of Death this weekend. To top off this day, my wife arrived for a day off together. I did not think she was coming this weekend until she called the last minute announcing she was on the way. Tomorrow is our 39th anniversary and we plan to spend it in Paris (Missouri, that is). I shall return to the trail then, continuing my journey across Missouri. I am in far better spirits than when I entered the state. Lots of this is because there is an angel back in Rochester, Indiana, who is using her phone to make contact with people before I arrive. Thank you, Shirley Willard—I see your unseen work and know you are there!

I'VE BEEN THINKING about angels today. By angels I do not mean the heavenly beings that are messengers of God, but *human* angels. When I hiked the Appalachian Trail, I first encountered these "trail angels." These are self-appointed folk who help out the many "thru-hikers" who are out doing the entire Appalachian trail in six months. Some of these Trail Angels lug coolers full of drinks out onto a hot mountain so that dry and thirsty hikers walk up to the "trail magic" quite unexpectedly. Others open up their homes to allow hikers to "crash" for a night and get a shower. A few of these are former thru-hikers "paying it forward" but most are just ordinary people who like to do generous things for others. I've encountered scores of trail angels on other hikes and this walk too. But beyond these along-the-trail angels there is that one lady back in Indiana I met only once who is constantly at work behind the scenes. Shirley's emails and phone calls are often behind the scenes working to make my journey more comfortable. How many times have I thought something good happened to me "coincidentally" when in fact this "angel of the Trail of Death" was behind it? Maybe this is the way real angels work too.

Father Benjamin Petit
Missionary to the Potawatomi Indians
Portrait by frontier painter George Winter

Day 43 Burkhart's Camp (Moberly, Missouri)—Mile 457
Oct. 16, 1838

ICE! When the Potawatomi woke this morning in Paris their water was frozen. Paris became a milestone of sorts for the emigration party. Until Paris the challenge was sun, heat and dust. Afterward it would become bitter wind on the open prairies, along with rain and mud. The Indians lived more by nature's calendar than printed ones. The first morning's frozen water indicated a change of seasons--a harbinger of the coming winter. It may have made them want to hasten their pace to get to the promised new houses in Kansas. Winter was coming! Breaking the ice on the water, they ate a bit, took down their tents and packed the wagons and horses—all of which took several hours each day, a wearisome task.

The group moved west in a cold wind for seven hours to Burkhart's camp—a few miles east of present day Moberly, Missouri. They would have followed the old "Bee Trace," a road at that time which connected the Mississippi and Missouri rivers across the state, generally the route of today's US 24. (Or perhaps a little closer to the old Wabash Railroad--now Norfolk-Southern). Indeed, for the last three weeks I have been crisscrossing the NS railroad route. That railroad did not exist in 1838 but it almost always follows the route and never "squares off" corners for farms. I've wondered if the railroad was built on the old "bee trace" right-of-way in Missouri but I am not sure yet. The road map from the period (showed to me by Nancy Stone, Monroe County historian) pretty well gave me an idea of the "roads" in 1838 so I have a pretty good grasp of the route where it follows or departs from 24. This section offered little water to the Indians and their escorts and thus required a longer than usual day. Jesse Douglass, the scribe for the official journal, reports "*Health still improving. Complaints of sickness are scarcely to be heard.*" It is a short entry.

Actually their probable "Burkhart's camp" was more likely near the present day town of "Old Milton" where they crossed the Elk fork of the Salt River. That camping spot would make true the journal locating the camp 18 miles west of Paris and 13 miles east of Huntsville. But the markers usually say "camped near here" and the Boy Scouts and historical societies have a gargantuan task of getting permission to place these markers and are often limited to city parks, rest stops and public locations. So they cannot always be put in the exact spot. One marker is actually located beside the men's rest room of a gas station in west Quincy--the only place that would give permission in the area for the marker.

AS FOR ME, Sharon left this morning after our day together. After someone leaves I am always more lonely. I'm headed west in a somber mood, knowing I will not see her again until the end of the journey. This day was a turning point for me too, but not regarding heat-to-cold changes. I noticed by the end of the day that I have quit counting UP my miles and have started counting *down*. I have come 457 miles so far. But I am now looking at a different number: I have 202 miles *left* to walk. At the same time I've noticed the people I meet have switched the opposite direction. When I started people were amazed that I was "walking all the way to Kansas." Now they more commonly exclaim, "You walked all the way here FROM Indiana?"

Today was a long one for me. The journal records their trip as 18 miles, and they took a direct westerly route, as I did. I went to the marker on a puddle-creek and knew the miles were wrong. Then I realized that actually they probably camped at the Elk fork of the Salt River 3-4 miles before I stopped--thus I put some extra miles in the bank for tomorrow. This night I was able to actually camp at the boulder-marker site—unusual for me since the spots are often in a too-public place to sleep. But I arrived well after sundown and one can lie down to sleep about anywhere after dark (assuming you also rise before sunrise, which I do).

I got relief from the sun this week, thanks to my umbrella. I had started off this trip with a Go-Lite umbrella and sent it home in the middle of the journey. I added the umbrella back to my kit this week. It is such a relief. I look absolutely silly walking along the road with an umbrella—as if I am some sort of blueblood walking with a parasol. However, in walking across the Mojave Desert last summer I discovered the great secret of walking with such "portable shade." I can leave off my hat and let my bare head catch tiny refreshing breezes on my sweat-dripping face. Even passing truck-wind was welcome today.

My progress this week will determine my ending date. Since I already have reservations to fly to Washington state June 17-24 I have to either finish this trek by the 16th, or come back and complete the final leg after a long-planned week in the Cascades. This week's progress will determine which will be my ending date. It is not up to me. It is a decision that will be made by my feet. The feet are the executive branch of a walker's bodily government. I can walk 25-30 miles a day with my head, heart, back and other body parts. The feet are always the weakest link. My blisters are healing, though 20-mile days on paved roadways adds new blisters on top of the old almost-healed ones. I have blister-layers now. So I will let my feet be the governors of my progress. They shall decide my actual finish date--and they'll decide that this week.

I'VE BEEN THINKING about assimilation vs. removal. What was the most pro-Indian position in 1838? It was *assimilation*? That's what the liberals then thought was the most "progressive" view. They wanted to blend Native American individuals into the American population by exterminating their culture. Save the individual Indian and kill the Indian culture. But the moderate position prevailed--*removal*. Give the Indians some land out west and let them alone forever. It sounded "reasonable" at the time. Indeed this was the "enlightened" view of people like Isaac McCoy, founder of the mission in Niles, Michigan. He believed removing the Indians away form the corrupting influence of white society was their salvation. Maybe it could have been better. The trouble was, we couldn't "let them alone." But at the time it sounded good.

Territory of Potawatomi at the arrival of Europeans

Day 44-45 Huntsville, Missouri – Mile 470
Oct 17, 1838

SNOW! The Potawatomi left Burkhart's camp with forbidding clouds in the skies and sure enough, soon after departing, at 8 a.m. snow started falling and continued all day. Jesse Douglas records it, *"...the snow commenced falling very fast and continued during the greater part of the day. Traveling was difficult, the road being exceedingly slippery, and the snow falling so fast as to render very cold and unpleasant the whole journey."*

How much accumulation of snow he does not say—but a "very fast" snowfall all day certainly would have produced a significant accumulation which would have made walking difficult and slippery. Imagine the cold feet and slush in the Indian's moccasins. Yet Douglas reports *"The Indians traveled without complaint"* adding that they *"seemed greatly to approve the exertion of government to place them at their new homes."* While we can easily accept the first half of this statement, the second half is a tad bit harder to swallow. Yet, considering the promises given, perhaps it was true. Hope dies a slow death. So does trust. They were to have houses in Kansas and the country was reported to be rife with game—a virtual paradise. I suppose we must remember that the whole country was moving west at this time—and perhaps the over-promising that was being done to whites in the east (and in Europe) was doubly done to the Indians? They still had hope that the Government would make good on its promises and this "emigration" forced-as-it-was, would be good for them ultimately. We have yet to discover if their hope was justified.

They slipped for seven hours to a camp near Huntsville, Missouri, a total of 13 miles for the day. After they pitching camp in the snow, during the night the snowflakes turned to rain. Imagine pitching a floor-less tent for the night where the Indians would sleep on the snowy-soggy ground then it turns to rain. At least Polke managed to purchase straw from neighboring farmers for them to spread on the icy ground to make their night more tolerable.

FATHER PETIT recorded this day as *"encampment in the snow"* followed by *"I am attacked by fever."* Petit was a sick man. He has experienced repeated bouts with "the fever" and each attack weakened him by increments as his resistance to future attacks diminished. Petit did not tell much about his own sickness merely listing it in his diary like he listed purchases. And he did not say much to his Bishop either. However, after the journey was ended when Petit was on his way home, he wrote his Bishop on November 26. Here he confessed with a more frank description his own difficulties on the journey. It is a picture of the sort of private difficulties that are behind his short entry confessing his attack by fever: *"Among the blessings which the good Lord granted me during the journey (I must tell you everything) were some tests of endurance: I was taken fever twice and I had an inflammation of one eye which for more than a month kept me from my breviary and made celebration of the Holy mysteries extremely painful and difficult. This inflammation of the eyes is an almost inevitable result of the dust, sun and wind in the prairies; several Indians even suffered from it. Then towards the end I came to a kind of exhaustion—without strength, without vigor. Today, since our arrival, I have been afflicted with fever again, and I cannot get rid of it, although I have left my tent for a house somewhat better, but even here one is occasionally too much exposed to the wind. The savages are going to build a hut for the Father and me, near the temporary church they have just erected; it will be more comfortable. I was so feverish that my body was covered with a kind of boil as large as one's thumb and in a state of infection which tried me so much that I was uncomfortable in any position.*

The next morning, (Day 45) dawned with continuing rain. Polke commanded a day off. As a result of months of drought, the roads were already covered with a fine dust, which the snow-then-rain turned to a mush making travel impossible. The Indians and their white escorts spent a cold rainy day huddled around fires and resting. The journal says, *"Nothing occurred during the day, save for the drunkenness of a few Indians who had procured liquor at Huntsville."* Once again, no matter how carefully the officers watched the Indians the "free market" prevailed and buyer and seller did the deal.

AS FOR ME "nothing occurred during the day" also. Since I had overshot their day yesterday, today's walk was fast--only actually being the last half of their day. I took the short walk from Moberly to Huntsville in a slight breeze that was much relief from yesterday. By 1 p.m. I was in the Huntsville library writing this journal. The day is still 85 degrees warm, but the breeze makes it tolerable and I shall push on soon.

I'VE BEEN THINKING this morning about ethnic cleansing. The term wasn't even used until the 1990's when it emerged as a description of the forcible population transfer of groups off their land. In its worst forms it involves a war with intentional destruction of the other race or tribe—i.e. "The only good Bosnian is a dead Bosnian." The phrase "ethnic cleansing" did not exist in 1838 but the action did. In 1838 it was called "Indian removal."

Day 46 Middle Chariton River, (near Salisbury) MO – Mile 481
October 19, 1838

After two days cooped up in tents sleeping on soggy ground, the Indians got up early today and were ready to move on quickly. By dawn the rain had stopped and the sky cleared though it was a cold day. The eleven-mile walk to the Middle Chariton River was without incident. The journal again reports the Indians *"to be anxious to reach their destination."* The journal says little more. They walked four hours to the river and camped. Lots of normal people's days are like this. You get up, do your thing, and then go to bed. On a long trek like this one many days will be filled with this "normal" kind of day. The only item that jumps out is the report that the Indians seemed "anxious" to get to their destination

AS FOR ME I am "anxious" too. After five weeks of steady walking I am like the Indians—I just want it to be over. As a gentle rain fell last night I found an obscure corner of a recently cut hayfield and fell hard asleep awakened only by periodic freight trains rumbling past my campsite every hour or so. I really intended to go further than I did but my feet refused. The debate went something like this:

FEET: "I'm stopping here, I've walked enough today."
HEAD: "No you're not—I'm in charge here—keep walking."
FEET: "You can be in charge all you want—but I'm not walking any more today."
HEAD: "I command you to keep going."
FEET: "Command all you want—I'm turning in to that hayfield to camp."
HEAD: "I am the head—I make these decisions."
FEET: "Sorry head—I carry you all day, and I'm done carrying dead weight."
HEAD: (To fingers) Don't you collaborate with him—don't touch those shoelaces."

The feet won. They are right about one thing. They do most of the work. It is one of the errors outdoor stores perpetuate—that a comfortable backpack enables a person to carry more weight. This is only true in the store. Out on a walk, the feet have to carry every ounce on the back no matter how comfortable the shoulder and waist straps are. I think half the bones in my body are in my feet—and most of them hurt.

I hurt. Sure, but compared to the Potawatomi the worst I experience is really only an irritant, not a real hardship. However, these irritants add up for a modern person like me who is accustomed to an easy life. Blisters are my chief irritant—they keep forming on top of old blisters-now-calluses. But there are other irritants. There is almost no place to sit down that is not infested with chiggers and ticks. Picking ticks off before they swell up like grapes is a constant bother, and scratching the chiggers on my legs is only reduced because I am too tired to bend over. The gnats are a regular irritant, especially when they insist on flying into the channels of my ear and then bouncing off the walls with their frenzied bussing. Worse than these are the gnats who nose dive (literally) up my nostrils on a Kamikaze flight toward my nasal passages. They always die trying but they still try. What is it up there they want? Mosquitoes are a bother mostly in the evening. My heal bones ache like a dull toothache—probably from the incessant pounding on hard surfaces. At night I frequently awake with a Charlie Horse revolt in my muscles. And I tire of being constantly soggy wet—drenched in my own sweat all day, sleeping in a soggy sleeping bag, and rising the next day to walk again with yesterday's leftover dampness still in everything. But I suppose the most nagging irritant is the constant tiredness that comes from a long trek like this. I just want to collapse in a heap on the grass somewhere and go to sleep for a week. A long trek has a way of wearing a person's energy down gradually until a walking pace by the end of the day is more of a stagger than a firm pace.

But all these are mere irritants compared to the Potawatomi's pain. I have little country stores every day or two where I get refreshed with nice food and a cold drink. I can walk up to any farmhouse and get fresh water that is safe to drink. I can even stay at a motel every week if I want to. And I do not have little children and grandparents along who are dying every day. Anyone who has ever taken a child to the mall to walk around knows that a child's ability to walk ten miles is rare. Certainly Indian children were no different. Lots of energy at the start of a day but in a few hours this energy runs out and they want to be carried. Did their mother or dad carry them? Did the Indians have permission to put their tired children in the sick wagons? Who knows? I just know that even with the relatively short miles the Potawatomi are doing in this section of Missouri, I am weary like they must have been. No wonder they are said to be "anxious" to get to their new homes in Kansas.

I walked this morning into Salisbury, Missouri by noon, in time for the library to open giving me access to my online pages. I find myself increasingly following the Potawatomi pattern of leaving early in the morning to get as many miles out of the way before the sun rises high in the sky. And the heat is only one reason for this; the second reason is that for westward walkers the afternoon sun shines directly into the eyes of the traveler. So I walk before sunrise until noon then find a shady place (such as this library) to hide out in until late afternoon when I return to the road for that most pleasant walking time of all—the two hours before and the first half hour after sunset. Thus I now have a few hours here to read in the local history section of this library of a town of about 1700 people.

While typing my day's journal the librarian slipped up and said, "Several members of the D.A.R and Museum board have gathered down at the Museum and want you to come down and talk to them." Then with a wink she added, "Small town, you know, everybody knows when someone new is in town." I spent the rest of the afternoon with these delightful women a decade or two (three?) older than me. They were full of energy and excitement for the Trail of Death, their genealogy library, my walk, and four full rooms of displays. After a long chat I received a personally-escorted tour of their museum with the story behind each item. I even got to see a quilt that was made before the 1838 emigration party passed this way, along with a variety of Indian artifacts that were made a thousand years before.

By late afternoon as the day cooled I headed out of town with rumbling thunder in the sky and severe thunderstorm warning blaring from my tiny radio. Then I spied a roadside motel of the 1950's variety. "Why not" I said to myself and entered the motel office-house of the owner. Looking around I asked, "Could I see a room first?" She agreed and I inspected room 17 which was "OK" (compared to the ground) and I checked in. It was a Spartan motel—a single thin bar of soap doesn't go very far for a walker who wants to bathe and wash all his clothing. But I rested OK and reveled in the 60 channels of TV--apparently more important than soap to the customers of this sort of roadside motel. I had the strange sensation I might be sleeping on the same sheets as my predecessor, but I didn't know that for sure—it just felt that way. This all made my night's sleep a bit restless. I kept feeling like I was being chewed on by little invisible insects, but it was probably all in my mind. At dawn I rose, walked back to Casey's country store for a couple cups of coffee, then headed west toward the Grand Chariton river and beyond to Keatsville, the destination of both the Indians and myself for the day.

I'VE WAS THINKING as I went to bed about the effects of injustice. There was an immediate effect—pain, grief, and death of some of the Potawatomi. But there are long-term effects too. When a nation carries out a sin against a minority, the effects can last hundreds of years. If my great-great grandmother had traveled this road, what effects might I be feeling today? Would I be tempted to hold a grudge against whites? Would I tend to distrust all whites still? I'm not sure how I'd respond.

Day 47-48 Keatsville, (present Keytesville) Missouri -- Mile 498
Oct. 20-21, 1838

After the recent snow, then rain, the roads were muddy today for the Indians and their escorts. The air was very cold as they covered the eleven miles from the Middle branch of the Chariton River to the Grand Chariton River in four hours (the location of their campsite is about two miles east of present day Keytesville, Missouri). The journal reports the health of the Indians as *"almost completely restored"* suggesting that there were less than a dozen sick Indians in the camp (though there were one or two of the officers who had been "indisposed" the last several days).

The subsistence was (as always) "beef and flour" which had been the daily fare for the Indians for the last 46 days. Jesse Douglas adds, *"of which the Indians are becoming tired."* Apparently it was difficult to get "bacon or pork" though there is some evidence that the white escorts may have gotten some. The militia had refused earlier to accept standard "Indian rations" as was the custom, and insisted on upgraded rations. The emigration almost always camped by a water source. Today's source was plenty large. I checked the depth and it was chest deep today—imagine the difficulty of fording it in the "Missouri muck" that forms the bottom of riverbeds. Even more difficult would be getting the wagons across without sinking into the gooey soil. 1838 was a drought year but during the previous few days the emigrating party had experienced lots of rain and snow so the flow of water may have been similar to what I saw. Whatever, there were no ferries on these "smaller" rivers. There was no way over them except through them.

The Potawatomi took all day Sunday off at the Grand Chariton River so the devoted Catholic Indians could worship, as was their custom. We do not know if other Indians joined in on the edges of these services or if any of the white escorts attended the mass led by Father Petit, but the attendance figures reported back at Logansport hints that some may have done so.

The big treat on Sunday for everybody was, *"During the day a considerable quantity of apples and cider was purchased and given to the Indians."* After seven weeks of mostly beef and flour (along with occasional deer meat) the fresh fruit and cider must have been a wonderful and healthy treat. Since they were traveling in September and October there would have been some remaining berries along the route but a "considerable quantity" of apples would have been a real boost to morale. Though one wonders how stomachs full of apples and cider reacted overnight.

AS FOR ME I walked early before the heat of the day from Salisbury to Keytesville. I saw the corn in one field that was chest high. I've been able to watch the corn grow as I walked--from Indiana's tiny half-inch sprouts on May 1 to this flourishing crop reveling in the same heat I am suffering from.

Today I met my first walker--he was headed east. It's interesting--in 498 miles of walking this was the first walker I've met (other than people walking on city streets). I crossed the road for a visit. I met Lee ("Everybody calls me Gator") Jackson who was out on his daily walk of 15 miles or so collecting aluminum cans ("They're up to 70 cents a pound now, you know.") He wanders the roads daily collecting cans to sell for recycling. "Here, want a cigarette?" he offered. "It's amazing what people throw out their windows," he remarked, citing a memorized inventory of things he'd found along the roads from hats, to screwdrivers, to jackets. "Last week I found a $20 bill rolled up like a cigarette beside the road" he reported smiling through his intermittent teeth. "I usually come back down the other side on the way home collecting the cans over there" he said jerking his head toward the side of the road I'd been walking on. "But, here, you want a sack to collect them yourself--they're worth plenty?" I declined both the cigarette and the sack and shook hands with Gator then headed west again impressed with his generosity. He was willing to share what he had, even share his claim on the westbound cans. The rest of the way into Keytesville I looked for cans and when I found them I kicked them up onto the shoulder of the road for him. I also secretly rolled up a few dollar bills like cigarettes and dropped them here and there with a chuckle. But I was not generous enough to drop a $20 bill. Now that I'm thinking back on it, I wish I had. I am in favor of a quarter or even half-dollar deposit on all cans and bottles. Not because it will reduce litter--it probably won't. But to enable people like "Gator" to get more than $4.00 for walking 15 miles picking them up along the road. People who get up off the couch and collect cans should be rewarded.

I am now sitting out the hottest part of the day in the Keytesville library (population 400). At the door I was greeted by librarian Ann Smith with, "You must be the guy from Indiana." I shall move west again and camp after the heat dies down in late afternoon.

I'VE BEEN THINKING about luxury liberals. By that phrase I mean people who are liberal or progressive but never have to pay the price for their views. When it costs us nothing we have the "luxury" of being liberal. For instance, the rich Philadelphia Quakers who opposed the Indian removals paid little for their position. If an Irish immigrant who was hoping for some rich Indiana land spoke up it was heroic. His convictions would cost him something. The rich Quaker in Philadelphia had the right position on matters like these, and they should get credit for being right, but they were mostly "luxury liberals." Their view cost them little in Philadelphia. I suppose the same thing applies for many Northerners who opposed slavery. However, when men in North Carolina stood up in their pulpits and preached against slavery (as the early ministers and members in my denomination did), they faced lynching and bullets in their church doors. How many positions do I have that cost me little? Many political positions are self-serving. For a rich man to call for lower taxes is not heroic. For a low-paid employee to call for increased minimum wages is not heroic. The Christian approach to many of these things should be more other-serving than self-serving. At least that's how it seems to me. I suppose I have plenty of "Philadelphia Quaker" views myself though—opinions that cost me little.

Keytesville city hall

Day 49 Grand River (Brunswick, Missouri) –Mile 514
Oct. 22, 1838

After passing through Keatsville, the party walked 15 miles to the Grand River just before it flowed into the Missouri River. They were at the river by 2 p.m. and began immediately ferrying the Indians across and had all Indians and many wagons across by dark. They were now in the broad flood plain of the Missouri-Grand Rivers. They camped immediately across the river intending to bring across the rest of the wagons in the morning.

AS FOR ME, I started early in anticipation of visiting the James Pecan Farm about a dozen miles west of Keatsville but alas when I arrived, they were closed. This part of Missouri is considered to be "Old Dixie." Southerners settled here after the War of 1812 and made tobacco the number one crop along with cultivating great pecan orchards in this area. In October when the pecans are ripe, it is a booming area with several on-the-road shops open. Today they were all closed as I headed into Brunswick where the Indians crossed the Grand River. In 1838 the Indians passed by were the pecan farms here? The pecans would have been ripe for picking for them—did they stock up? Were the pecan farmers generous?

Brunswick was not closed, it was just busy. Busy Brunswick. Everyone in the town was busy and I was not noticed or seemed to be an intrusion. I had entertained the thought of a night in a hotel here, having heard there was one in Brunswick in the original house of the city's founder. A homeowner who offered water outside of town had said the owner was "kind of interesting." When I approached the small hotel, the owner was on the front porch wildly tearing away at a two-liter bottle with a Bowie knife turning it into tiny shreds. "A recycler," I thought to myself, approving his behavior, thinking even more positively about stopping over. I stood unnoticed on the sidewalk watching him work furiously tearing the bottle into tiny shreds. Then, finished with his work he tossed a quick glance my way, then stood up and flung his 12-inch Bowie knife with all his might at the sidewall of the porch where it stuck deeply into the wood. It landed right in the center of a human outline marked on the wall. I decided to skip the hotel night after all.

Brunswick people were busy. From all my walking I've noted there are two ways of saying, "May I help you?" One reflects a tone of a sincere offer of help. The other uses a tone, which has a subtext saying "Yes--what do you want—I'm busy here so hurry up and tell me so I can return to my work." It is this second response I kept getting in Brunswick. Nobody was mean. Nobody was harsh—they were just busy. I was an interruption. At first I attributed it to an isolated instance when I encountered this response at the Casey's General Store, but I also got that sort of response at the dime store and gas station. Then I met a similar response at the grocery store, and even at the library where two women were shelving books and made it clear I was unwelcome today: "We're really not open today" though I was already inside. I sighed and walked on. They returned busily to their work. At the edge of town I found a newly-renovated B&B but I walked past—no reason to stay longer in this busy town. Perhaps it was just me. Or the weather. Or happenstance. Or maybe they only treat walkers like this and go out of their way to make driving customers feel welcomed. Or, maybe they are hospitable only by appointment, like some families are. If I had called ahead I might have received a friendly welcome. Or maybe this only happens on Thursdays. Who knows? I walked on.

I pitched my tent under a large water tower in the country. In most Midwestern towns a water tower indicates a town so I have often been able to judge how far away the next little town was. In this part of Missouri that doesn't work. Water towers are found in the middle of the country as often as in towns. Someone somewhere along the line committed the area to providing rural water service to every farm. Water towers like the one I'm sleeping under dot the landscape. Tomorrow I shall go to Carrolton and I am told there is a motel there—I might get another motel night tomorrow night.

I'VE BEEN THINKING about friendliness. I know that Shirley Willard and her auto-traveling tour were showered with hospitality in Brunswick so they must be a friendly people. Not to me. Oh well, who knows? But now that I'm thinking about it, I've seen churches like this. They can be extraordinarily friendly at one time and to some visitors, and then completely ignore others. I've seen busy churches too. Their programs buzz like a well-oiled machine. They have carry-in dinners, youth programs, quilting bees, and ministries to retirement homes. Yet when a stranger walks in he seems invisible. I'm thinking tonight about the "hitchhiking vacation" I took with my high school son John. We were hitching cross-country while sleeping under bridges and in old barns like tramps (it was his idea of an adventure). On one Sunday morning we decided to attend the first church we saw open. Thumbs out we tried to hitch to the next town. We got no rides from the nicely dressed people passing us. Sometimes they waved. After eight miles of pounding the pavement we arrived at Centerville Nazarene Church. We slipped into the second from last row. During the greeting time one lady recognized us as and as she pumped our hands apologetically exclaimed, "If I'd known you were coming to church, I'd have picked you up."

Day 50 Thomas' Campsite, (near DeWitt) Missouri --Mile 536
Oct. 23, 1838

The party got the remaining wagons over the Grand River by noon and headed ten miles away from the Missouri bottomlands, recording in the journal *"the bottom lands of the Missouri being too flat and wet to encamp upon an hour longer than was essentially necessary.* They marched three hours and camped at what they called "Thomas' Encampment." The only other entry of interest for this day was about food: *"Subsistence beef, flour and corn."* So far on the trip they had repeatedly listed beef and flour daily but here the journal adds corn, which had only been listed as forage for the horses. Was this a slip of the pen or did they add corn or corn meal to the Indian rations? The last week of October was probably too late for fresh corn. The horses were fed "corn and corn fodder" so certainly corn was plentiful in the area.

AS FOR ME I walked this day as the second part of the day before.

I'VE BEEN THINKING as I go to bed about our "dangerous world." I am constantly asked by folk if I am afraid of "weird or dangerous people." They seem disappointed that I have no story to tell of crazy axe murders out looking for walkers to kill. Generally they tell me that they think I'm brave to go out without a car. I am already being warned of "walking through downtown Kansas City alone." So far I've been urged to get a police escort and others have suggested having a white person tail me in a car. Really?! Why is everybody so afraid? I think it is TV. Each night they watch news programs that train them to think the world is full of crazy people and life is very dangerous. I have not found this to be so at all (Then again, I'm not watching TV and have not done so at home for almost five years.) Fear sells. News programs don't report, "Almost a million people in our city went to work today and nothing much happened." The reports, the headlines, the music are all designed to create a sense of panic—life is dangerous! It must work—everyone thinks I am brave by merely walking on a public road in the United States of America. Phooey! The people who drive cars while using cell phones are in more danger!

Day 51 Carrollton, Missouri –Mile 536
Oct 24, 1838

The most shocking entry of all appears in today's journal. To me, at least. They walked a dozen miles into Carrollton in the bitter cold on the open windy prairie. Here is found the casual entry in today's journal: *"This morning before leaving camp a quantity of shoes were distributed among the indigent and bare-footed Indians, the weather being too severe for marching without a covering to the feet."*

Can you believe this? Had some of these Indians come 536 miles in *bare feet?!* This was not merely an upgrade from moccasins to hard shoes—the journal specifically cites the Indians' "bare feet." Incredible! Maybe their moccasins had worn out recently and they had been in bare feet for only a few days? Or had some of the Indians walked more than 500 miles in bare feet? It is common in other ancient cultures for children of poor people to walk bare-footed until they become adults. Was this the case for the poorer Indians here? Were these children? If so, no wonder so many kids gave up and died at the end of the day. Sure, Indian feet were hardened, but still, did some of these Indians walk 500 bare-footed miles? Perhaps it was only for a day or two. Even so, for a walker like me, that itself is a painful thought.

And, where'd they get the shoes? Did they have them all the time in the wagons and were hoping to not have to issue them in order to avoid straining the government's budget? Did they buy them in Carrollton? How many extra shoes would a shop in a tiny town have in 1838? Or, had they been buying them up as they went along the route and just now were distributed them since it was getting so cold? What about last week's snow? Did Indians walk bare-footed in that snow? Incredible!

Some have theorized that all the Indians rode horses or rode in the wagons for the entire journey after Indiana's General Tipton left. Tipton did claim to have recommended this to Polke in order to shorten the trip. This may have been partially true. Petit reported the Indians had 250-300 horses, and a carriage was provided for the chiefs. There were forty baggage wagons in which the equipment along with the sick, women, and children could ride. Did some Indians walk the entire distance without riding horses or in the wagons? Petit had described riding in the wagons as insufferable—choking the riders with dust and sun baking them like a dusty oven. And even riders on horses often got off in those days to "rest" by walking. And at least one older Indian claimed in Logansport he had never ridden a horse and wasn't about to start now—he planned to walk all the way to Kansas. Did he? How many walked the entire route? We do not know. But today's entry shows that at least some Indians were walking 500+ miles into the journey—and they were doing so bare-footed.

Today's journal also mentions the Mormons for the first time. Missouri in 1838 was the location of the infamous "Mormon Wars" between the settlers and the Mormons. The Mormons had established their settlement in Missouri (as they had before in Illinois before being kicked out of that state) but the settlers wanted them out of Missouri too, and hostilities arose including armed troops, cabin-burning and outright warfare on both sides. The journal reports it this way: *"The country through which we passed today is very much excited. Nothing is heard—nothing is talked of but the Mormons and the difficulties between them and the citizens of Upper Missouri. Carrollton is nightly guarded by its citizens."*

The Indians were removed because they were in the way of "ordinary people" (i.e. white European settlers) who wanted their land. The Mormons were white and European, but they were "in the way." In their case it was religious differences, not racial ones that brought about their removal. Mormons had not been welcome in Illinois. They were not welcome in Missouri either. Having been expelled from both states, they would go west until they found land nobody else wanted.

AS FOR ME I spent most of the day thinking about the Mormons and the Indians and their similarities and differences and the fate for both groups whose paths almost touched here in Missouri in 1838. But mostly I thought about shoes. I am on my fourth pair of shoes and I cannot even imagine walking one day of this journey in bare feet—let alone 51 days in a row. Maybe none of the Indians did that either—maybe their shoes just recently wore out. But the entry seems so unbelievable to me today—even if they only walked a few days bare-footed.

I walked into Carrollton by noon and found a fairly new motel about a mile north of town to spend the afternoon and night in. While shopping in the Country Mart grocery store the manager asked, "You walkin' across America or something?" I told him what I was doing and he inquired, "You like fish?" I assured him I liked anything edible. He disappeared to return with a huge Styrofoam container packed with cooked fish with "no charge" written on the top. When I got to my room I partnered the fish up with a loaf of bread and several cans of cold corn for lunch and dinner combined. Full of food I simply lay down like an overfed lion and slept while the TV played in the background. By bedtime I felt like I had actually already had a day off, though in fact I had already walked a full Indian day from dawn to noon. I enjoyed my life of leisure so much I tried to add a second night (Saturday) to my "weekend off" but the hotel was already filled up with what the desk clerk called, "old people coming back for a class reunion." I moved on.

I'VE BEEN THINKING today about suffering. I'm especially thinking about the Catholic Church and Christianity and suffering. Christianity has at its core a story of suffering—the cross. It is a story of a man submitting to suffering and injustice without complaint: "as a lamb to the slaughter." Christianity prepares people for suffering and supplies stories and models for help in handling it. This is I suppose good, since life is full of suffering. The Catholic branch of Christianity is even better at emphasizing this suffering motif than Protestants. So I'm guessing the Catholic Potawatomi had a *via dolorosa* model already imprinted on their minds. They knew how to handle injustice and suffering with faith and courage. However, some have accused Christianity (especially Catholicism) of collaborating with injustice through this approach. They have accused the church of pacifying the common people, training them to suffer injustice and abuse at the hands of the rich and powerful and to do it like Jesus, without opening their mouth. When this happens, they charge, the church becomes a collaborator with the rich and powerful, keeping the poor and disenfranchised in their place. Is this true? I think there is some truth to this charge even if it was never the intention of a church. A Christian leader must walk a fine line. There is a time to submit to suffering as Jesus did. There is also a time to rise up and address power and wealth, insisting that what they are doing is wrong and won't be taken any more. Father Petit tried to walk this fine line I think.

Day 52 Snowdens, (near Richmond, Missouri – Mile 561
October 25, 1838

Today's march was probably the longest mileage to date—perhaps 25 miles but we don't know for sure. It was the first day in the journal that the mileage was not listed –just "*an unusually long journey*" and the campsite was "*near Richmond*." and Father Petit has an entry titled "*Richmond*" in his daily diary. The emigrating party considered this campsite adjacent to Richmond wherever it was. The marker is located in town by the Richmond high school, but the markers are placed at sites where permission can be gained and almost always refer to the camp as "near here." It was south outside of Richmond I think, if the journal mileages are accurate.

From tomorrow's journal we know they made it to the Missouri river in two hours (again for the second day in a row the journal does not list the miles). The party so far has been traveling at 2½ mph (or occasionally as fast as 3 mph), which means they must have camped on a radius of six miles from the Missouri River crossing at Lexington. I think it may have been somewhere around present day Henrietta where there is a permanent water source (Willow Creek). We know they camped near "Snowden's farm" so research still to be done may show exactly where this Snowden's farm was located and how close to Richmond it actually was. If it is anywhere near the high school, the time for the following day may have been listed as shorter than it really took, which is quite possible.

Perhaps it was the furor over the Mormons that made them forget to list the mileage. Soon after camping a delegate from nearby Richmond came to Polke to request he join them with his militia to protect Richmond who were expecting an attack from the Mormons that night. Polke declined, explaining he had a federal assignment he could not abandon—removing the Indians to Kansas.

FATHER PETIT was waiting in his tent to begin evening prayers on this day (or maybe a day near this) when two young Frenchmen showed up at his door. They spoke little English and had boarded a steamboat to get to New Orleans and the ship's captain had dumped them off at Independence telling them they were at their destination. They were now walking to New Orleans and, passing the encampment dropped in. Petit reports it to his Bishop this way: *"These gentlemen spoke and understood very little English; this made their position difficult in this distant land. While passing along the road, they had seen our tents and fires. 'Perhaps it is a fair," they had said to each other, and, curious as all Frenchmen, they had come to see. Then, very much*

127

surprised to hear some half-breeds conversing in French, they had spoken to them, and, learning there was a French priest here, they had themselves brought to me. I greeted them as well as possible. We spoke of our country; I invited them to supper, following which they attended public prayer with much edification. They went a little way off to retire. They were somewhat frightened by the state of the countryside, which was all in arms. The majority of the Protestants in the country had resolved to exterminate or at least expel certain sectarians called Mormons, who had refused to submit to the tax and the public charges." In a short entry in Petit's daily diary he simply said, *"American army forming at Richmond—Cannon and rifle fire without seeing the enemy."*

Here we get a glimpse of the "Mormon wars" from a Catholic point of view. Catholics sometimes taunt Protestants when they get alarmed at new sects rising that depart from orthodoxy. Catholics sometimes say that the constant splintering of the Protestants was an inevitable effect of the Protestant Reformation. They see the Protestant rebellion against the Pope as launching the notion that any group or nation wanting to found their own brand of Christianity can do so. Catholics warned such Protestant rebellion is a "centrifugal force" and would eventually spin off a thousand denominations and independent churches that cut themselves off from external authority. They warned that all kinds of cults and sects leaving orthodox truth would occur sooner or later using the "Protestant Principle." Most Protestants now admit this. But the Mormon wars were not just a religious matter. True, both Protestant and unbelieving Americans rejected and persecuted this religious group who practiced polygamy and held beliefs beyond orthodox Christianity. But there were political factors too. While there are some similarities between the treatment of the Potawatomi and the Mormons, the Mormons were well funded, well armed, and were quite capable of launching their own attacks on villages which they did. They had done just this exactly ten days ago. On October 15 one hundred Mormon volunteers had plundered and burned the town of Gallatin, Missouri. Tomorrow the state militia would be called to battle against the Mormon fighters and after four days the Mormons would surrender and promise to leave Missouri after the coming winter. Eventually they would travel to Utah and occupy "land nobody else wanted"—something they had in common with the Potawatomie Indians.

FATHER PETIT described the battle zone to his Bishop: *"...the next day we heard artillery and rifle shots. We saw armed troops coming to formation from every direction, about sixty mules—booty taken the day before from the Mormons. We passed quietly through this theater of fanatic battles, although at our arrival a message had come asking that the Indians join the troops* *who were attacking the Mormons. This request was wisely rejected."* Polke had about fifteen "dragoons" or volunteer soldiers in his party along with various other officers, interpreters, and staff, plus the civilians who were driving the 40 carts and carriages—perhaps there were a total of 75 white men. Seventy-five white men with guns could have augmented the Missouri Militia considerably, but if they could add in a couple hundred of the Potawatomi braves on horseback it might have resulted in major boon. Petit reports that they were not recruiting the whites this time but the Indians. He also reports that Polke wisely refused.

AS FOR ME I walked from Carrolton in two days reversing my sometime double-days of the Indians by halving their long day. The journey took me across billiard-table flat bottomlands of the Missouri. I camped at an abandoned farmhouse halfway across the bottomlands. In fact for more than 20 miles there was only one actual farm where I could ask for water—the rest have been abandoned, perhaps bought on by huge agribusiness enterprises that make their millions on federal subsidies that purportedly protect the "family farm?" Or maybe nobody moved back here after the floods of 1993? For me it made for plentiful campsites under the remaining trees, but spaced far my sources of water. I walked by thousands of acres of future Fritos, Karo Syrup, and Corn Flakes growing as high as my head now. Overnight a great storm moved in dumping four inches of rain on my tiny tarp-tent but I stayed dry though damp, as always.

I'VE BEEN THINKING about "evangelism" tonight. I have been turning the clock back 400 years before the removal—to the time when the American Indian had never met a white man. I've been playing this mental game all day. How would I "evangelize" these Indians if I had been here first? I've been pretending that all day. I've imagined myself "evangelizing" the Indians. They already believed in God, accepted the afterlife, took on the discipline of spiritual fasting, and were a people of prayer. They believe God sometimes spoke to men in visions or dreams or especially while fasting. How would I approach "evangelism" of these people? Finally I solved the puzzle with a simple substitution. I asked myself how I would have "evangelized" Abraham or Isaac if I could have somehow traveled back in time. When I imagined how I might "witness" to Abraham, I somehow came to see exactly how I'd approach those Native Americans. I'm still thinking about it. Oh well, only insiders—regular churchgoers--would understand the idea of "witnessing to Abraham" so I quit thinking about it, and I probably won't write this in the final book. (I did.)

Day 53 Lexington, Missouri – Mile 566
October 26, 1838

In a short two hours the party made it to the ferry crossing of the Missouri River at Lexington. By 10 a.m. they were crossing the wagons, as usual leaving the Indians on the opposite shore from town. All that hampered them was *"we found the ferry fully engaged in transporting females who were flying from their homes. Reports are rife throughout the country of bloodshed, house-burning, etc. The people seem completely crazed."* Apparently the woman and children were fleeing the region, allowing the men to stay behind to fight the Mormons. But the Indians and their escorts did get all the wagons but a few across by dark leaving the next day to complete the ferriage of the Missouri River.

FATHER PETIT inserts a confusing paragraph in his letter to Bishop Brute at this point. Right after describing the Mormon conflict, Petit described walking along the bank of the Mississippi River. Petit next wrote: *"As long as we marched along the left bank of the Mississippi, the heat was excessive, the weather sultry, the water bad. On the opposite bank the temperature was cooler—sometimes becoming even cold—and this change produced happy effects on the health of the Indians. After arriving in Missouri, we had hardly any sick."* It is not clear to me what Petit meant. First, after the Mormon incidents they crossed the Missouri River, not the Mississippi River. Perhaps Petit mixed up the two rivers in his letter to Brute since they did not march along the Mississippi at all, but quickly walked away from the water to escape what seemed to be dangerously wet bottomland. Perhaps he simply switched the rivers in his letter. If he did he may have also switched the banks too? The south side of the river (left bank) would have offered far more protection from the sun than the north side. Indeed I had a similar experience after crossing the river at Lexington and walking down the left bank of he Missouri. That was one of the most beautiful and shady sections on my entire walk. More study is needed on what Petit was reporting here and if he mixed up the sides of the river like he did the two rivers themselves.

AS FOR ME I got in high gear today. It was cool with a strong breeze blowing so I walked into Hardin, then Richmond and then all the way to Lexington anticipating the "weekend" of a full day off that I've not had for a while.

As I crossed the Missouri I remembered my 1999 canoe trip. I traveled by canoe the entire Missouri River that year from its source at Three Forks, Montana to St. Louis. That trip included a stop at Lexington. This is the first time in all my trekking that I have ever crossed a former route—Appalachian Trail, Pacific Crest Trail, Colorado Trail, Missouri River... this is the first "intersection" of two treks. What I remember most from that canoe trek was the abject loneliness I felt for so long. That's one thing I like better about this walk—I meet people every day—friendly and interesting people.

I had to walk three miles past Lexington to find the motel and when I found it, I registered two nights. I first went to the large "Lexington Inn" but found it abandoned with grass growing everywhere. I next asked a lady on the highway if there was any other motel in Lexington to which she replied, "There's a little brick one across the river run by foreigners—if they're there." Sure enough, I found a brick 1950's style motel operated by folk from India. (They have operated it for 27 years—I wonder when they will no longer be considered "foreigners" by their neighbors?). No pool, no phone, all smoking rooms but I was happy that it was suitably clean and I determined to have a full day without walking—all day Monday.

My trouble was that the library and post office were three miles away, a six-mile round trip. However the owner of the motel offered his van and the motel handyman drove me into the library reducing my six-mile trip to a mere three mile return trip—merely enough to keep my muscles warm now. I already walked the extra three miles south getting to the motel last night, so all I have back to the route now is three miles.

The new bridge across the Missouri has bypassed traffic around Lexington. It will hurt this town I suspect. Stoplights and narrow roads make for off-the-cuff stops and that is what keeps towns like this afloat. I hope people come on purpose. Just watch how friendly the people are—even if you are a walker. And that's saying something since people are naturally suspicious of walkers.

At the post office I received more than 30 pieces of mail! Whoa! Some of them had bounced up to me four times as they skipped across post offices like a flat stone skips across a lake—now they caught me. As I promised, I have answered every one. I love this town. The librarian greeted me happily. The Mexican restaurant was delicious. The postal clerk was gracious. The town has more than 25 *benches* all around the sidewalks expecting people to rest and relax. As I answered my letters on one of these benches eight—e*ight!*—people slowed down and greeted me with a friendly hello... and then only one person, the ninth, walked past without a greeting. Lexington is a town that has not yet been Wal-Martized. You can still buy things in the town—things like shoes or furniture or office supplies. It is only a town of 5000—yet has a six-plex theater. What a delightful clean and friendly town! I decided to stay in town all day and not return to my motel until dark, and when I started the three-mile return trip a state police car picked me up and hauled me back to the motel—the first time I've had a state police car respond to my thumb. Though he could have been checking me out.

I'VE BEEN THINKING about the death of small towns. On this walk it seems like I've passed through a hundred of them already. They all follow the same pattern and their ghosts all look alike. There is an old abandoned hardware store, furniture store, drug store and a few other unidentified storefronts. All of them are empty and full of dusty stored rubbish from the last occupant who tried to make a go of it there. The post office is the last to go. If there is a store still breathing, it is usually a pizza store or a bar. After that, a tiny bank might still be open. If there is anything else, it is sometimes an antique store trying to make a go of it on the weekend traffic. I expected more of these leftover teeny towns to have gas stations than I discovered actually having them. Apparently a gas station needs a fairly large population to support it. If there were a larger store it was a Casey's convenience mart on the road outside of town. Sometimes I sit in these ghost towns and pretend I hear sounds from other generations. They are like nursing homes—there is still life around but you know the final expiration is approaching. Seeing a town that has survived this has raised my spirits today.

Day 54-55 Little Schuy Creek, (Wellington) MO -- Mile 574
Oct. 27, 1838

As soon as the Indians ferried across the Missouri River, they were hurried through Lexington and on their way, causing the column to spread out along the shore of the Missouri as they headed to Little Schuy Creek for the night. The front part of the party reached camp by 4 p.m. but the rest of the column must have straggled in hours later making the total miles for the day eight.

They camped two nights here since they had permission to not walk on Sundays so the Indians could worship. However worship was not the only order of the day on this Sunday. In the morning chief Ash-Kum headed a delegation of Indian leaders to the headquarters, protesting the "*unrestricted power by I-o-weh whom they did not choose to acknowledge as a chief of the blood.*" This is not the first time a rivalry had emerged among the chiefs, not uncommon in the white man's dealings with the Indians, usually to the great disadvantage to the Indians.

The second issue they raised was their promised annuities. As part of the purchase and settlement with the Indians, the government promised various short or long term annual payments. Polke "*hoped they would cease to speak of a subject which could not be of benefit to them*" and apparently avoided addressing the matter. Did Polke know that the too-often practice of the government was to walk away from such deals eventually--sometimes right away? Is this why he avoided speaking? He was not an Indian agent and there is some evidence he thought this whole affair was questionable. If so, was he wagging his head inside at the whole affair? Did he know that the government almost always abandoned their promises? The trouble was that the Indians took a verbal promise to be binding. The government considered only written promises to be binding--and even the written promises were often discarded "because the situation has now changed." I wonder what Polke knew this morning when the Indians, now approaching their new homes, asked about their payments. As always Polke solved a diplomacy crisis with tobacco--he offered some "in hopes that they would continue in peace and harmony." He did tell them he knew of their annuities but did not act as an agent in the matter, presumably leaving that up the their new Indian agent in Kansas. Polke later would write that General Tipton had made these promises to the Indians. I think when Tipton burned the Potawatomi village he may have assuaged the Indian's shock by promising "the government" would build replacements in their new land. To the Indians a spoken promise was as good as a check. This check would bounce.

The journal reported the sad news of the day: "*A child died in the night some time--the first for the last four weeks.*" It was inaccurate—a person had died 16 days ago, but who was counting? Many of the children were already dead. After this child covered 574 miles he or she finally gave up and passed away. Sad.

AS FOR ME I got a great boost this morning. Kerry Kind, an old friend who is a minister from Indianapolis, showed up at my little brick motel room announcing "I'm going to walk with you a couple days." Kerry had gotten into his car at sunset the night before and driven all night to catch me before leaving Lexington's only motel. We drove back into Lexington where we asked the city police where to park his van a few days. We got invited into the early morning coffee-break briefing of the city's police force. Parking the van right outside the police department, we headed west down the delightful and historic route 224, walking almost all the morning in 100% shade with cool breezes blowing on us as we walked along the Missouri River, chatting and theologizing together. The miles flowed fast as we talked and soon we were passing the party's Little Schuy campground before we even had our first sit-down break.

I'VE WAS THINKING TODAY about road kill. I know it sounds silly, but I've walked 575 miles through America's heartland and my most constant roadside companions are dead animals. I wonder if there have been studies done on how many creatures are dispatched annually by automobiles. I sure see a lot of death on the roads. From my own informal survey I'd say the most common death on the road are birds—about a third of the dead bodies I encountered are birds. I am a bird watcher so I've identified more than twenty species so far. It is a sad find. After the birds are mammals. I'd say about a quarter of the bodies are possums—I can't believe there are that many possums. Perhaps their nocturnal habits combined with a slow gait makes them easy targets for automobiles? After possums I've seen almost everything else: fox, coyotes. bobcat, deer, squirrel, groundhog, rabbit, along with the normal amount of pets—mostly dogs and an occasional cat. And after these there are the snakes and turtles. In all these cases I usually can smell death before I see it. Every time I smell it I think of that Bible verse about the smell of death, but I's too tired to remember tonight where it is or what it actually says. I'm just going to sleep.

Day 56 Prairie Creek, (Near Buckner) Missouri --Mile 584
October 29, 1838

Today was a quick four hour/ten mile day for the Indians as they moved west along the Missouri River to camp at Prairie Creek (now Fire Prairie Creek, near Buckner, Missouri). Presumably the day had started with a funeral. If the child who died through the night was under the care of Father Petit there would have been a Catholic funeral and Pastor Petit would have consecrated the ground where the child was buried.

The journal reports the food as "*flour, corn-meal, beef and pork and game of every kind.*" They were eating better now. The Indians had gotten tired of flour and beef long ago but now we see that they did indeed have *corn-meal* along with *pork* and *all kind of game*. This may be a point to remind us all that the Indians probably hunted and gathered food every afternoon and evening. Seasoned backpackers might wonder why they walked only 4-5 hours on many days but the Indians spent much of the afternoon hunting, and gathering firewood along with setting up their shelter, so stopping by mid afternoon in late October was sensible.

At five o'clock Captain Hull came into camp with 23 Indians who had been left behind five weeks ago—the first week in Logansport. This small party of Indians and their escorts had remained behind until they got well, then traveled more than 500 miles trying to catch up with the main column. This may also remind us that the official death count (42) does not include the deaths of those who had escaped the party (more than 100?) nor does it include any deaths of those who separated from the party and traveled on their own. The journal reported the condition of these 23 as in "*tolerably good health and spirits*" but says nothing about any dying. My own hunch is there may have been a dozen or more other deaths among the escapees and those left behind or traveling separately, but I can't prove that.

AS FOR ME, my new companion, Kerry Kind helped the miles fly. Not only because of stimulating conversation but because he insisted on carrying my tent, making my own load lighter. He said he had two days to ruin his feet, then he'd go home and I had to keep walking so he'd help that way. Since I still have a healing silver-dollar blister on one heal I accepted. What a friend! We walked on along the river through the triple towns of Wellington, Waterloo, and Napoleon (I'm serious). We took a wonderful rest at the U.S. Army Corps of Engineer's headquarters for Kansas City where I was interviewed for yet another newspaper story. We clipped along past Prairie Creek and headed toward Buckner, hoping for a place to eat.

Today was only the second time I was kicked off a resting spot. We spied a delightful shade tree 25 feet off the road near what appeared to be a pay-to-fish pond so both of us sprawled out under its shade only to be sighted by a woman 100 yards away who said nothing but repeatedly gestured, "move along" with her hands. We complied without arguing, putting on our sweaty not-yet-dry socks as she stood with one hand on her hip and the other gesturing us to move along each time we looked her way.

By dusk we arrived in Buckner, Missouri, just ten minutes before their Misty's restaurant closed. Kerry reminded me that if the woman had not shooed us away from her grass, we would have arrived after the diner had closed. Thanks to the shoo-away lady we ate well. We both feasted on a meal I thought I'd never forget (though I already have by the time I am writing this down). When we had finished eating our meal (accompanied by the heavy scent of Pine-sol as they mopped the floor), it was almost totally dark. We slipped across the street to the edge of town and pitched the tarp-tent behind an apartment building in a little playground. This sort of "stealth camping" seldom bothers people—coming after dark—leaving before sunrise. Kerry did not even bring a sleeping bag, sleeping all night in just a thin jacket.

I'VE BEEN THINKING about country people. I have always had the impression that "country people" are friendlier than city people. I have found that to be untrue on this walk. Most everyone has been wonderfully friendly and helpful to me but in the few cases where I have been treated less well (most not reported here) it was in the country, not the city. Each time I've had the cops called it was by country folk. At no time did a person in the city ever shout at me, or pull the drapes back and refuse to answer the door. I wonder why this might be true. Could it be that people who live in the country don't have a close neighbor to call out to? Do country people feel more exposed? Lots of people walk around in the city, but a walker in the country seems suspicious, I suppose. Maybe the reason some country folk live in the country is to get away from people and this is why they install long driveways? I don't know, but my experience on this trip has made me wonder if there have been any studies done on this.

Day 57 Blue River, (near Lake City) Missouri -- Mile 598
Oct. 30, 1838

The Indians were marched five hours today from Prairie Creek to the Blue River (probably present-day "Little Blue" river, east of Independence, Missouri. The atmosphere was jovial as the Indians visited and caught up with the 23 friends who had arrived last night. The party of 23 Indians had among them three wagons transporting all their earthly possessions (and any sick people) and only five horses. Today this group was officially attached to the main column under Judge Polke. Hull had left Logansport on September 27, 1838 and caught up during this final week here at Blue River. (Jacob Hull's day-by-day journal is skimpy—usually only one line per day—but provides additional insight on the route taken by both groups.)

AS FOR ME I am cruising with Kerry. Once again we put in a "double day" covering two of the emigration party's days in one day. We walked toward Independence by hiking a five-mile leg then took a break, then another five miles of walking, and so forth all day. This is the mile-eating regimen backpackers use on log treks and it can run up 25 miles of hiking with only four breaks a day—walk five miles then eat breakfast; walk another five to lunch, walk the third five to afternoon break, then another five to dinner, and a final evening five to bedtime. Of course when backpackers do this they are often seduced into walking another 1.2 miles to get a "marathon day" of 26.2 miles. This is exactly what former student, Mark Schmerse and I did through most of the state of Oregon on the Pacific Crest Trail in 2003 when we walked from Canada to Mt Shasta in California—1150 miles. But now I am on paved level roads, which should be easier than high altitude trails, but isn't—at least not on the feet.

Day 58 Independence, Missouri --Mile 608
Oct. 31, 1838

Passing through Independence the column camped just two miles below the city. They made ten miles for the six-hour's walking, slower than usual. Perhaps walking through Independence slowed them down. A hint of this comes at the end of the short entry for the day: "*Many Indians came into camp during the afternoon much intoxicated.*"

Once again they handed out shoes: "*in the evening a small quantity of shoes were distributed among the emigrants.*" Perhaps they had purchased these in Independence. In 1838 there was not yet the mass production of shoes or a "shoe store" that would carry a large stock of shoes. So, presumably these shoes were purchased from the town's cobbler? Or, from individuals? Were some used shoes? Were they buying shoes right off people's feet? Or were the shoes already in the wagons from the beginning? Who knows? Once again, we do not know if the Indian's moccasins had worn out and they had become bare-footed, or they had been walking bare-foot all along—just that they distributed a "small quantity of shoes."

FATHER PETIT made the first entry in the last six days in his diary today. His last entry was made in Richmond almost a week before. At this town he wrote, *"Independence, frontier town—wine and letter from Vincennes."* They were reaching the ends of civilization, as they knew it, Independence being on the edge of the so-called "Indian territories" to which they were going. Petit does not say who sent the wine from Vincennes though that was the seat of his Bishop so perhaps his superior sent the wine to him with an accompanying letter. Was it to become consecrated wine for the Eucharist or some "wine for the stomach's sake" for personal use? Perhaps both. We do know from his later letter that Petit was weary and sick, daily losing strength and vigor. He may have simply been too weak to do much more than survive the day's miles and ministry to the Indians—he could have simply collapsed into bed after his duties were completed which is why he had not been writing in the diary. I can only guess.

AS FOR ME I camped about where the Indians had camped—two miles south of the old center-city Independence, though my campsite was a motel-- since I am now walking through completely built-up cityscape. On arriving at the motel, Kerry called a local Wesleyan Church pastor who cheerfully offered to take him back to Lexington where he had parked his van. We Wesleyans have a network of reliable helpers just like the French Catholics priest Petit did. Kerry and I gave a quick man-hug-goodbye to each other and

I went to my room and to sleep before sunset. Together we had walked more than 40 miles in two days and I had gotten a good rest for my feet with Kerry's tent-toting. I'm closing in on Kansas.

I'VE BEEN THINKING about littering. The trip must be getting near the end—my mind is wandering to all kinds of insignificant subjects—like road kill and the trash I've seen along the highways. It is funny—when I buy a soda in town and drink it along the highway I carefully tuck the cup in my pack until I get to the next town. Yet the liter bugs that could easily put their trash beside them in a car and wouldn't have to carry it—toss it out along the road. Beer cars and bottle are by far the most common containers. The "open container law" may have actually contributed to this trash. I've passed thousands, maybe millions of beer cans and bottles. Are there really this many people drinking alcohol in automobiles? Again I am reminded of my hope for a 25-cent or even half-dollar deposit on these—glass and aluminum are virtually everlasting along the road. It would either end littering or help the poor—either way our culture wins. As for paper trash the winners are fast food cups and sacks, and after that cigarette packages, and those little round snuff containers. Actually I've gotten good at "reading the trash" almost like reading tealeaves. Within ten miles of the next town I know I am going to have a McDonalds, Casey's, or a Sonic in that town where I can get some food. The drink containers appear first, meaning they last the longest. As I get closer to town, sacks of fast-food garbage show up—apparently people eat their meals first, toss out the sack, and then finish their drink. I sometimes think I ought to pick up this trash—but I would quickly fill a second pack in a few hundred yards. Some states have heavy fines for littering, but laws do little to control what people can do in secret. Driving a road where there are no cars or houses in sight is private behavior in America. So drivers toss out their garbage. I've found all kinds of interesting things along the road too. Sometimes I try to imagine the story of how it got tossed out the car window. "Girlfriend takes boyfriend's cell phone, finds number in address book of competing girl, rolls down window and angrily tosses phone out the window." Or, "Those sunglasses make you look like a retired woman dear." Or, "So, you don't like that music–well I wouldn't want to listen to anything *you* wouldn't like, your majesty." On some days I have invented 25 different stories like this and I laugh aloud at them as I am walking. I am either getting bored or going crazy.

Day 59 Blue River, (Near Grandview) Missouri --Mile 624
November 1, 1838

Many of these Indians were devout Christians. Not all of them, but many were. Indeed, they were probably more devout than their escorts. We already know that they had a full multi-hour mass on Sundays and had requested no travel on Sundays for religious reasons. However, the journal generally ignores these religious matters. But, in today's official journal we catch a glimpse. It says the party *"left camp a little after 9--one hour or so having been allowed for their religious exercises."* What is this? It was a Thursday, not Sunday—what special services were these? Father Petit's letters indicate a virtual flood of services, sometimes all night as they sang hymns and prayed. He also tells of how he officiated at the funerals. And, every day they had morning prayers and evening prayers. This was a worshipping community of faith being removed to Kansas. They were Christians—from all the evidence more devout Christians than their escorts. But we still are not told why they delayed their departure an hour today for today's service--were these some special services? The answer is probably found in the Christian calendar: today is All-Saints Day, a high and holy day preceded by "all-hallows-eve" (our present Halloween). All-Saints day is not just a Catholic day—it was one of John Wesley's most hallowed days. I am guessing The Indians had a special service to celebrate All Saint's day.

They traveled 16 miles and almost crossed the state line today. Food and forage for the animals was in abundance and they were happily anticipating crossing the state line into Kansas and what the maps would label, "Indian Territory." (If they only knew.)

It is worth remembering that the Indians ate more than their distributed provisions. They probably spent the afternoons and evenings hunting game and gathering berries and roots. While the Indians got rations of beef and flour and occasionally pork, apples or other food, they much preferred wild game and gathered food. Petit described this to his Bishop: *"The Indians were permitted to hunt on the way, and from the Illinois River almost to the limits of the Indian Territory they destroyed many deer, turkey cocks and pheasants in a magnificent hunting ground."* Thus the prisoners of war gathered plenty of their own food. The richness of the hunting must have encouraged the Indians as they headed west. However, as they continued west it was less encouraging. Petit follows the above line with, *"But we had the misfortune of finding that in the outskirts of the country assigned to them game became scarcer and scarcer, and no woods were seen other than little clusters on the banks of brooks which flowed far from each other in these* *vast prairies."* The Woodland Potawatomi were accustomed to hunting and gathering from the woods, so being forced to leave woodlands and relocate to the prairies was perhaps the worst sentence of all. It robbed them of their ancient style of livelihood and made them more reliant on government annuities. They knew how to survive in the woods, but life on the prairies was a sentence to Siberia. There loomed ahead of them a lot of hunting in their first winter in Kansas, but with little success. They would often be hungry.

AS FOR ME I rose long before sunrise intent on crossing into Kansas. Heading for Grandview, I was delayed only by a Kansas City TV interview with Martin Augustine—a reporter who was not just making a story to "fill up the news hour" but was genuinely interested in this story. He even walked a good distance with me, not just as a photo-op, but several *miles*! His film crew kept leapfrogging and filmed us walking, then me alone repeatedly as I walked toward the "State Line road" where one side of the street will be Missouri and the other Kansas.

I'VE BEEN THINKING about tribalism again tonight. Indian culture was tribal. It still is in many ways. That is, rather than thinking of themselves first as Indians, or as Native Americans, many think first of themselves as Potawatomi, Navajo, Ute or Blackfoot. Many tribes also are divided into "Bands" and some of these Bands dislike and distrust other Bands even in their own tribe. Some hardly speak. And, there is not one person who speaks for all Indians. Still. This is why it has been hard to decide on matters like sports team mascots—one Tribe condemns the action while another applauds it. As soon as someone speaks up against Indian injustice some radio show host will find another Indian somewhere who says the opposite. While the Europeans were accustomed to have a king or President who purportedly spoke for all people, the Indians had no such unifying authority. It occurred to me today that in this, Native Americans are like Protestants. We too have tribes and bands and denominations and no single spokesperson. We even have some denominations that hardly speak to other ones. The US government used Indian tribalism to the Indian's disadvantage. If the Indian agent could not persuade the existing chiefs to sign a treaty they often found more cooperative Indians who would name themselves chief and take the signing bonus. Tribalism (and "denominationalism") has value, but can be easily used by enemies. (Or *the* Enemy, in the case of the people of God.)

Day 60 North Fork, Blue River, (near Stillwell) Kansas --Mile 636
November 2, 1838

Even though the day was rainy-miserable they set out anyway. Polke was anxious to get there. So were the Indians, so they moved in spite of the rainy conditions. Once they started moving, the rain did not slow—it increased. In an hour they crossed out of the "United *States*" and into Kansas, "Indian Territory."

As soon as the party crossed into Kansas, "civilization" disappeared. Roads evaporated. And it was raining. The rain would make it hard to follow the "trace" or faint path of the wagon wheels. They were traveling on the open road-less prairie. At noon a large portion of the party on horseback lost the trace of the wagons that had traveled there previously and wandered about for four hours on the prairies, lost. There were more than 300 horses so this must have been a soggy mess. Finally they found the trace again and caught up to the wagons. They camped at the North Fork of the Blue River--their third campsite on one or another of the forks of this river. The journal-writer then records *"having traveled a distance (it was computed) of twenty-five miles."* This is one of the rare instances where the Jesse Douglas, the scribe, uses the term "it was computed" to refer to miles. Perhaps this figure includes some of the wandering to find the lost trace and Douglas was not with that group? We do not know, but it is an unusual phrase this day and probably means something. This 25-mile figure probably included the wandering and may have been the miles of the last group into camp—the lost group. They left this morning at 8 a.m. and record coming into camp at 3 p.m.—a total of seven hours travel. Their usual 2 1/2 miles per hour rate would get them 17-18 miles assuming the rain did not slow them down. If they equaled the best time ever of 3 miles per hour, the seven hours could have gotten them 21 miles, thus the 25 miles figure likely includes the wandering. The cumulative miles figure I have listed at the head of this entry does not use the 25-mile figure but uses the actual miles from the last camp to this one, which is 12.

AS FOR ME I walked down the state line road until my time ran out, then turned west and walked into Overland Park, Kansas, and slept beside a creek located behind a Cineplex 16 movie theater. Zoning is so strict here that they must have "set-asides" for natural areas because I chased away several deer while setting up my tarp-tent. While they have zoning for natural set-asides, they apparently have none requiring sidewalks in this expanding community—I am walking mostly in the street or on the grass. Having walked the miles of another "double day" I dropped off asleep by 8 p.m. rising at 5 a.m. and went along searching for coffee. I was quickly rewarded.

Walking into Olathe, Kansas, I found Mid-America Nazarene University where I checked out the story that ran last night on KMBC-TV. The Librarian here was delighted to let me post these reports and is now trying to arrange my travel to the airport to meet Sharon who is waiting in the state of Washington for a week of previously planned vacation in the Cascades. I am only two days from the end of this journey, but airline reservations are made and are as rigid as waiting wives-on-vacation, so I must leave the trail so near its end and come back in a week.

I'VE BEEN THINKING about walking. I'm not thinking so much about my walking on this trip as walking *itself*—ordinary walking. The world is no longer made for much walking. It is made for driving. New sections of town seldom have sidewalks—they just assume you will drive a car if you want to get a cup of coffee. Springfield was my worst city of all for this, though these new sections out from Kansas City are a close second. All this reminds me of some of my students who I've actually watched come out of their residence hall, start their car and drive it two blocks to their classroom. Two *blocks*! Maybe these students were raised on the edge of town like this where there were no sidewalks.

Day 61 Bull Creek (Paola) Kansas –Mile 651
Nov. 3, 1838

Traveling six hours the party came to Bull Creek where a settlement of Wea Indians was located (near present day Paola, Kansas). The journal reports the Indians anxious to be finished with the journey and to meet with the Potawatomi Indians already resettled there by previous removals. The mileage was not reported today but might best be calculated at 15 miles based on the locations of the two campsites and their travel of about seven hours.

The journey would end tomorrow so the officers tried to take a census of the Indians to satisfy the military's record-keeping penchant. Tomorrow they would be reunited with other Indians and sorting out the exact number in the emigration would be more difficult. They made little progress. The journal puts it this way: *"During the evening an attempt was made to enroll the Indians, but not very successfully. They did not seem (or would not) to understand or appreciate the object."*

Tomorrow was Sunday and they had been promised no traveling on Sundays. The chiefs may have sensed Polke would try to travel on Sunday, or perhaps they overheard a discussion. Whichever, late on this Saturday evening several of the chiefs came to Polke requesting that the Sunday day-off promise be kept. Not only did they want to worship, they may have wanted to get cleaned up and prepared to meet their friends already at Potawatomi Creek just eight or so miles ahead. Polke denied their request, agreeing only to allow for a two-hour delay for their worship services.

FATHER PETIT received Father Hoechen's visit today, just one day from the end of their journey. He reported to his Bishop: *"At a day's journey from the Osage River, Father Hoecken, of the Society of Jesus, came to meet us. He speaks Potawatomi and Kickapoo. He announced his intention of leaving Kickapoo's country, where he has resided, to establish himself among my Christians."* Petit had been instructed to accompany his parishioners to their new homes and accomplish a handoff to the Jesuits and this was to be his successor. Father Christian Hoechen was a 28-year-old priest and had been helping Father Van Quickenborne in his Kickapoo mission which had produced meager results. He was being transferred to the Potawatomi. He would become instrumental in establishing a new mission with the Potawatomi, as we shall see. At this point he is just their new priest—there is no church, no parsonage, and no mission. Though it would be several weeks before Father Petit would start his return journey to Indiana, on this day the turnover to his successor began. The reference to the "Osage River" is a mistake. Perhaps the emigration labeled the water Osage for the "Osage River *Indian agency*" The actual Osage River is at a distance.

AS FOR ME I returned to this trail after a week off in the Cascades with my wife. I was anxious to finish the trail. Taking a red-eye overnight flight, then renting a car, I drove to the trail where I left off the week before stashing the car and walking briskly south until past dark. I walked down Rt. 169, an Interstate highway wannabe, almost to Paola. I heard of only a "slight chance" of rain so I left my tent in the car, chancing the final might on the trail would be clear.

The "slight chance" turned out to become about an inch of rain in a one-hour downpour. Luckily I was near buildings and slipped under the protection of a drive-through portico of a day care center for rich kids located at the far edge of suburban Kansas City. Sleepy from the airplane night, I fell asleep on the concrete entryway; awaking an hour later to an evening's clear skies. Refreshed, I walked another eight miles making the total for the day almost 20 miles. I was as anxious as the Indians to be finished. I slept on still-wet grass near a tree nursery under open skies without my tent, crossing my fingers for no more rain.

I'VE BEEN THINKING about ending this walk. For two weeks I have been pondering the appropriate way to end and have had two ideas. The first decision I made was to finish alone. Various folk offered to come and finish up with me or to plan a ceremony or celebration. I decided this did not fit. Only a person who had walked this distance can understand what it means to finish such a walk and celebration is out of order for me—as if this walk is an "accomplishment" of some sort. It should end more like a funeral than a victory party. I want to *mourn*, not celebrate. I'd feel like an outsider at such a ceremony. Actually, the Potawatomi who originally took this journey are the only ones who know what it was like. They are all dead. And my walking didn't even get me 10% of their pain, probably less. I can't grasp what *they* experienced. Others can't grasp what I have experienced either. People who lived in air-conditioned houses and drove around in cars the last two months shouldn't be present when I finish this journey. I need to be there alone.

My competing thought has been to NOT finish at all. The longer I've walked, the less I feel that I have a right to be the first to walk this path since 1838. Who am *I*? Shouldn't it be a *Potawatomi* who first re-walks the entire 660 miles, not a white man? Or at least it ought to be a Potawatomi and a white together that walk it? I have thought of walking 10 miles short of the ending point then stopping and waiting for whatever number of years it takes for a Potawatomi to catch up then I'll walk the final leg together with him or her. Is there a Potawatomi who would do this? Who? It has been almost 170 years since the original journey and none have done so. Shouldn't there be at least one Potawatomi who would remember the courage and faith of their ancestors by walking this route? How soon? In the next ten years? Has a Potawatomi already walked it and kept their journey secret? What if one decides to walk it in 15 years. Will I be too old to finish with them? These are the thoughts on my mind now. I must decide in the morning, for tomorrow is the last day's miles. I will either stop here and go home with an unfinished walk, or push on to finish the entire journey alone. I shall sleep on it.

The woodland Indians were unaccustomed to the open prairie

Day 62 Potawatomi Creek, Kansas Mile 660
Nov 4, 1868

Today they delayed departure two hours so the Catholic Indians could worship, perhaps with the joint team of Father Petit and Father Hoecken presiding. They ended their 62-day journey with the eight or nine mile walk to Osawatomie, Kansas from Bull Town. Here they found "Potawatomi Creek" where they were to be deposited and *"welcomed by many of their friends."* The journey was over. The Indians had been "relocated." "Removed." The journal-writer tried to put the best light on the Indians' response saying, *"The emigrants seemingly delighted with the appearance of things—the country—its advantages—the wide spreading prairie and the thrifty grove, the rocky eminence and the meadowed valley—but particularly with the warm and hearty greeting of those who have tested (and but to become attached to) the country assigned to them by the Government."*

The journal over-estimated their positive response. A speech would be made by chief Pe-pish-kay (which is recorded in the official journal putting a different light on their response including the following: *"We have been taken from our homes affording us plenty, and brought to a desert—a wilderness—and we are now to be scattered as the husbandman scatters his seed."* Pe-pish-kay's speech probably better represents the Indian reaction than the "spin" in the official journal. However, credit is due to whoever included the summary of the speech in the journal. My hunch it was at the direction of Polke that the scribe summarized the oral speech and included it in the record.

The mileages are confusing. Again today the journal-writer uses the cryptic words "The distance of to-day's travel is computed at twenty miles." There is hardly any campsite on Bull Creek that would produce a 20-mile journey to Potawatomi Creek at Osawatomie, Kansas. Probably this day produced eight or at the most nine miles. It's odd. The mileages have been meticulously recorded for six weeks then in the final days they got sloppy, either forgetting to record miles at all or listing longer-than-possible miles according to their time traveled or the geography. In the cumulative miles at the top of this entry I have used the nine-mile figure which is about as far as the distance can be stretched.

The journal curtly reports, *"Mr. Davis, the [Indian] agent, we found absent."* We can imagine how Polke and the militia felt about this. They had traveled two months to deposit 700-800 Indians into the hands of the Indian agency and the agent was not even present. Pe-pish-kay noted the same in his speech the next day. The Indians wanted to assess what sort of man they would now be at the mercy of. Polke they knew and trusted, but they knew nothing of this absent Mr. Davis. Indeed, they pled with Polke to stay with them until Davis showed up. Polke could not, having to go back to Independence to report on the successful mission, but promised to leave his son with them until the agent returned. We do not know how this turned out. Did Polke actually leave his son? Did Polke return? There is no record and my answer to the question (or yours) is based on an assessment of Polke's character. I tend to believe that he kept his word. However, there is not enough evidence to say either way.

As for numbers, we do not know for sure how many Indians arrived. Father Petit told his Bishop *"The number of Indians at our departure was about 800. Some escaped, and about 30 died—I do not think their number exceeded 650 at their arrival."* Petit may have been underestimating on all points. The official journal lists 43 deaths, (perhaps 44—it is not clear how the child that fell under the wheels of the wagon can be counted). Petit's death count is low, for certainly the official journal would have greater interest in underplaying the number of deaths than stretching it. Maybe Petit was listing from his own records and not counting the Indiana deaths before he caught up to the Indians in Danville. From the official records we are led to believe there were 859 Indians rounded up at Twin Lakes and when put with the 650 arriving one can see why the route became known as the "Trail of Death." For a long time it was widely believed that 859 Indians left Twin Lakes and only 650 arrived—leaving more than 200 dead. The name is so well established now that any attempts to change it to "Trail of Courage" or "Trail of Faith" are like changing the name of a familiar street or city—it confuses things. It is now remembered especially for the number of children who died along the way—a trail of death for children. We do not know for sure how many Indians escaped along the way, perhaps as many as 100-150. And, some of the deaths were newborns that came into the world on the journey, so they were not counted in the number leaving. A perfect figure is difficult to make. Petit's 650 figure for those arriving may also be low. Many of the marker stones along this trail list the number as "about 800 Indians" which may be fairly accurate. Did others die who are not recorded in the official journal? Undoubtedly. The journal tended to ignore deaths that took place among those left behind for several days to recover—that is, it only recorded deaths of those in camp and on the march, so that would account for some other deaths, though we do not know how many. I think about 750 Potawatomi arrived.

FATHER PETIT's assignment was over. He had faithfully handed off his congregation to the care of the next priest. In closing his report to his

Bishop, he encapsulates a pastor's work by saying, *"Thus, Monsignor, your aim and mine have been achieved. This young Christendom, in the midst of the anguish of exile and the ravages of epidemic, has received all the aid of religion. The sick have been anointed, the soil which covers the ashes of the dead has been consecrated, faith and the practice of religious duties have been maintained, even in their temporal sorrows he whom these poor people call their father has had the consolation of often being able to render assistance. And now left in the able hands of the Jesuit fathers, they need not regret the violent blow which has torn them from us—from the country, and they say, where their fathers rest—to leave them once more in the hands of the same priests who, more than a century ago, established traditions so favorable to Catholicism in the heart of these tribes. You wished, Monsignor, only for the glory of God and the salvation of these Christians. I looked for nothing else. Let us hope your wishes will be fulfilled."*

No pastor who loves the flock ever leaves easily. Petit had heard the call to U.S. "missions" in France and taken the risk of traveling to a strange and wild country where few spoke his language. He had applied himself and learned enough of the difficult Potawatomi language to serve as an interpreter—even to deliver some sermons without an Indian interpreting for him. His chapel constructed lovingly by the Indians and his cabin had been torn from him and handed over to white people who occupied it by the "law of pre-emption" that allowed them first rights to Indians' properties by moving in before the Indians had vacated. He had suffered with them as he traveled without complaint. Now his mission was being turned over to another priest. He was now to await his next orders—which he already knew would tell him to return to Indiana. What would be his next mission? There were a few remaining Potawatomi in Indiana with whom he could use his language skills. Where would his Bishop send him next? Thoughts like these must have been on Petit's mind as he awaited his next letter from the Bishop. Whatever, he knew it would not be with his beloved Potawatomi congregation—they were in the hands of another now. He had done his job as pastor and the time for his departure had come.

Petit was paid by the government for his work as interpreter. His daily diary lists a receipt of $245 as his salary. Petit had taken a vow of poverty so he couldn't keep it—it was the church's. He was able, however, to use church money for living expenses hence his careful recording of all income and expenses as a matter of accountability to the Bishop. The $245 did not stay with Petit's long. On the same day he spent $224.50 of it on the following: He lent $100 of it to Father Hoecken to buy a wagon and a pair of oxen, presumably to establish the new mission. He bought the doctor's kitchen utensils, perhaps to use on his journey home or for the mission, or more likely to give to the Indians. He paid nothing for his tent—he demanded the government make a present of it to him, and Polke did. He exchanged his big gray mare for a *"horse which will stand the winter better in Indian fashion."* He lent another $30 to Bourassa Lazare for his return costs and this loan was guaranteed by Abraham Burnett. Petit spent little on himself, and at the end of the day had less than $25 left.

The official journal continues for several days beyond this Sunday arrival. On Monday it records Pe-pish-key's speech and the Indian's request that Polke stay with them. Polke promised to leave his son behind in his stead while he returned to Independence to finish up the paperwork and report on the journey. It also records the death of an old man. One of the most surprising reports in Monday's journal is the arrival of a wagon belonging to Andrew Fuller, a Potawatomi from Michigan who had traveled all the way on his own, bearing all his own expenses for the trip to be with his Indian tribesmen. Here is a wonderful example of tribal loyalty—if a tribe was being forced to move west, Andrew Fuller and his family would go too—even at his own expense. The Indian's anxiousness to arrive was replaced on Tuesday by the anxiousness of the militia to depart. They wanted to get back to Indiana and their homes. It was the first week of November and if their journey home took two months they would miss Christmas. However, they were a small party and probably could make it by late November—"Thanksgiving" didn't yet exist at that time.

THAT'S THAT! The Indians were simply "dropped off" at Potawatomi Creek near present Osawatomie, Kansas, with a still absent Indian agent and no actual houses for them. Certainly Polke and his soldiers' thoughts turned to home the moment they turned their faces east. However they must have felt like a father who had just dropped off the sick family pet in the country. The Indians had been "in the way of progress." Something "had to be done." Removing them all to the "Indian territories" was the nationally agreed-upon and widely popular political solution for the "Indian problem." There! That's that! The Indian problem was solved. Indiana only had to clean out the remaining pockets of Indians and it could become, "the land of the free and home of the brave." *Really*? The Miami Indians and others would soon follow. Indiana would soon be fairly "cleaned" of Indians and the white Europeans could have "their" land free and clear. Out of sight out of mind. No longer would they have to see the poverty of the once-proud race of Indians. No longer would drunken Indians in their towns bother them. The Indians were largely expunged from the state—though it would retain the name Indiana –"land of the Indians."

AS FOR ME I decided this morning to finish my walk all the way to the end. I decided that I am not taking this walk representing the Potawatomi—only a Potawatomi can do that. I am not even walking this route as restitution or penance for white people—most whites don't even care about this injustice and I can't do their penance for them anyway. I am taking this walk *for myself.* It is my own way of trying to connect with what happened 158 years ago. It is my own form of penance. I represent nobody but me. So I shall finish. Today. Over the last few weeks various ideas have come to my mind for finishing. Now I've settled on a three-point plan and I shall write the closing sections of my journal using those three points.

My Physical Ending.

Rising at 4 a.m. this last week of June, 2006 I am soaked from the night fog, but knowing I would not be using my sleeping bag tonight, it doesn't matter. I walked into nearby Paola then on the Osawatomie and found Potawatomi Creek where I sat on the bank trying to feel what the Indians might have felt. I felt mostly relief. Relief that the hard journey was over. Maybe that's all they felt too? I also felt *grief* for the dead children buried along the way. That has haunted me more than anything. And I carry a sense of injustice and anger at the whole affair. And also, perhaps a feeling of *resignation*—a sense that power and the lust for land had won over justice and goodness. It always does (for the time being). Resignation that many of these Indians were headed to become wards of the state, children hidden in the back closets of the country. I was not jubilant at finishing this walk, only sad.

The first of my concluding ceremonies was to bury a physical item in the creek bank. I dug a hole with my hands for the precious arrowhead given to me by Josephine Gander, which I had carried all this way. It belongs here, not in my living room. It came from the soil on the Trail of Death. It belongs in the soil at the end of the trail. The ceremony was not fancy--just a simple affair that was perfectly suited to reflect how this whole unseemly affair itself had ended—they simply dropped off the Indians, then headed home to Indiana. Covering over the arrowhead and tamping it with my foot into the soft creek bank, I turned back to town and hitched the 30 miles north back to my rental car because I had two more personal ceremonies to end this trip properly. To do this I needed auto transportation.

My Spiritual Ending

The second place I had to visit to end this trip was 20 miles south of Osawatomie. In an hour and two quick hitches I got back to where I had parked my rental car two days before. I then drove back south to Osawatomie, then 20 miles beyond it, where I knew the "spiritual destination" of this journey was located.

The Potawatomi did not stay at Osawatomie. The promised houses did not materialize and the prairies were not even broken yet—let alone tilled. This would not be the final time the government's promises would turn to sand. The bitter cold prairie wind came soon after their arrival. By Christmas they were shivering and cold and felt abandoned by the government. As the bitter cold swept in they decided to relocate to the St. Mary's Mission just 20 miles south of them. Here was a band of about 150 Potawatomi that had moved one year earlier. On this smaller band's arrival they had sent for a priest. Father Christian Hoecken responded who had been working with the Kickapoo tribe with slim results. He founded the St. Mary's Mission at Sugar Creek. By March most of the Potawatomi had relocated from their drop-off point to Sugar Creek, thus joining the Indians who had been living there already.

Here they found a refuge—a fresh flowing spring, a small creek and plentiful rock formations in the creek's ravine where poles, blankets and bark could be arranged to provide protection from the bitter prairie winds and snow. Besides Father Hoecken and some lay missionaries, the Indians were most influenced by a devoted nun, Rose Philippine Duchesne. The Indians called her *"Woman-Who-Prays-Always."* Mother Duchesne was a Mother Teresa to these Indians.

Philippine Duschene had been called to missions as a young person. She had grown up in a wealthy French lawyer's family, and then heard a Jesuit missionary speak about evangelism. She immediately felt called to missions—to evangelize in America. She joined a religious order but her missionary call was delayed by the French revolution, which outlawed organized religion of her type. Even when she could again publicly practice her calling she was delayed again. Finally at age 49, (1818) she was sent as a missionary to the recently acquired Louisiana Territory. She arrived in New Orleans and worked her way up the river.

When the opportunity came to join the new mission to the Potawatomi at Sugar Creek, she had her lifelong calling fulfilled—working with the American Indians. Here at the St. Mary's Mission she ministered to the Potawatomi through prayer and service. Soon a small town grew up that including a chapel, blacksmith shop, a school and eventually houses. The Potawatomi practiced their devoted Catholic spirituality though not without opposition. Within a year, two traders from Logansport (the Ewing Brothers) sent employees all the way to Kansas and set up a trading post so the Potawatomi did not get beyond the evil influences of white civilization for long. Liquor became so available that the priests at the mission led a kind of bottle-smashing crusade reminiscent of what would become the temperance crusades of later years. Since whole books have been written on the Sugar Creek Mission I will not tell the whole story here, having previously restricted myself to the 62 day journey in this record. The story is powerful, the devotion of the missionaries inspiring, and the devoted response of the Potawatomi is moving. I had to go to this place to end this walk. As for Mother Duchesne, the *"Woman-Who-Prays-Always."* she never could learn the difficult Potawatomi language, which is perhaps why she gave her ministry to praying for them.

AS FOR ME I drove my rental car to this out-of-the-way site—the *Philippine Duschene Memorial Park*, which is the spiritual terminus of the Trail of Death. Charismatic and Catholic Christians along with Native Americans think there is such a thing as sacred places—places that offer "holy ground" where one is drawn closer to God. Some Christians feel that way about trips to the Holy Land or old Camp Meeting grounds. I had heard of this place from Shirley Willard and several Native Americans who had been urging me at every mail drop to visit it. Sure enough, it was a powerful and intense experience for me.

Here I walked among the rock formations where the Potawatomi huddled that first winter. I saw the location of the chapel and foundation of the cabin of Mother Duschene. I lay on my back staring at the seven crosses raised on the hill with the inscribed names of all the Indians who died and were buried here.

But I knew where I would be moved most of all so I saved it for last. Near the spring is a stone monument where a summary of the entire diary of the 1838 journey is inscribed. I sat and read. Day by day I re-read the journal I had been living with for two months. I recalled day by day the events of the Indians I had pondered so long. *Logansport* where more than 300 were sick. *Danville-Jacksonville-Quincy* and a dozen other memories I had of the Indian's journey. I had a picture in my mind of each entry. I had walked that path. I recalled the river crossings. I remembered where they got rid of General Tipton, where Father Petit arrived, where they hunted for game and "filled the camp with venison." Where it rained, when it snowed, where they were issued shoes, where they smoked a keg of tobacco, where they argued over the power of the various chiefs.

I sat for hours as the sun sunk in the sky reading and re-reading this journal and pondering all the memories I had re-created of the 1838 journey. They flooded back. I merged with their story memories of my own journey: rainy days, mental and physical exhaustion, blisters and the people—Nikki Mountain family's care for me, of Don and Liz Gander, the dinner at Josephine Gander's house, Steve and Janet Tieken, Phil Woodbury, Brooks Sayer, Jason Dennison, Mark and Jess Schmerse, Kerry Kind, and a score or more of others who faithfully sent letters and snacks to my mail drops along the way. I recalled them all tied in to the proper journal entry on the stone monument. The Potawatomi memories mixing with my own memories--1838 with 2006 and they became one.

The sun sank out of sight and quiet darkness crept in as I pondered both journeys: the Potawatomi's and mine. I know I can never completely feel what they felt. I'm a modern white man. It can't happen. Yet living with this story for two months as I took the actual steps every day experiencing my own blistering heat and chilling rain has helped me catch a bit of what they experienced. At least I understand it better than I could have sitting in an air-conditioned office reading a book about it. I know what happened was wrong. Not just wrong, *sin*, *evil*. And sin should not be dismissed lightly, even the sins of our forefather's government.

As the final glow of the light leaked out of the sky I reluctantly left the park. I headed out to complete the third leg for ending my journey, that involved reconciliation and forgiveness.

My Relational Ending

The final leg of my conclusion involved people. Having walked for two months (May and June, 2006) with the ghosts of the Potawatomi Indians, I wanted to complete the trip with real Potawatomi Indians—living descendants of those original Indians who walked the Trail of Death in 1838.

The first Potawatomi I met in Kansas City. Daniel Bourassa was probably in his 40's when he walked the Trail of Death with nine members of his family, including a son in his 20's. Though his family experienced the hardships of the trek, all of them survived according to family oral history. My first contact with a descendant was with Peggy Kinder, great-great-great granddaughter of Daniel Bourassa, along with her mother and her two sons—three generations of survivor-descendants. She had found my blog on the walk and had written several times to me at mail drops inviting me to meet her family. I now showed up. Peggy and her family are Baptists, which is the Protestant stream in the Potawatomi story. Though the Baptists sent no missionary on the Trail of Death as the Catholics did, the Baptist stream still flowed from the original Potawatomi—right down to Peggy Kinder.

Here I saw a copy of a hand-written Potawatomi dictionary now in the Smithsonian, which was written by Joseph Napoleon Bourassa, the son of Daniel (and Peggy's great grandfather). Even more impressive was the hand-written book she produced which he wrote, that was packed with medical treatments and healing recipes of his day. This is a matching book to the one in the Smithsonian. Peggy's mother Elizabeth told family stories of the journey passed down through the generations. Peggy and her family had just returned from an Indian gathering that week in Oklahoma. We ended the day with a taco dinner accompanied by Peggy's husband, mother and the children.

This happy laughing family dinner brought a sense of completion to the journey for me. I was not alive in 1838 and my own family was still in England at the time, yet I feel a sense of responsibility for what our government did to these Indians. I needed a reconciliation of sorts. Peggy and her mother were so open, so generous, so loving and forgiving that I stayed until dark. When I left I had a small sense of reunion with the past—with those ghosts I've walked with the last two months. What could I apologize for? Andrew Jackson, General Tipton and others? But somehow fellowshipping, eating together brought a sense of healing to me. They treated me as a family member—as if I was some distant uncle come for supper. At dark I headed west where I shall meet the other family tomorrow.

For my final connection I drove 150 miles west into Kansas—to find the descendants of *Equakesec* (Teresa Slaven) who was about seven years old when she traveled the Trail of Death with her older sister who was about nine. The family does not know for sure if they traveled with their parents or if their parents had died in a plague and these two little girls were cared for by others in the tribe. We do know that these little girls survived the 660-mile trek west when so many other children had died. Indeed the nickname for little surviving Teresa was "Living" since so many other children from that journey are dead and buried in the unmarked graves on the trail.

Why I had to drive so far into Kansas to find her descendants is yet another story of abuse and injustice to the Indians—one I am not primarily telling in this tale. The Potawatomi did not stay at St. Mary's Mission south of Osawatomie long—only a decade. Then the government got new ideas and moved them again—this time to a new St. Mary's Mission in what is now St. Mary's, Kansas where still another Catholic mission and school was established by the devoted priests and nuns. Here in St. Mary's I found the descendants of little survivor Teresa.

I found not just one descendant but a whole family! A *big* family! I had received several letters at mail drops from Sister Virginia Pearl, a nun in mid-Kansas, who had invited me to meet the descendants of little Teresa. When I contacted her she immediately commanded a family reunion of sorts so I could meet her family. I spent the afternoon and evening with this laughing-loving family and it was a powerful tonic. Here I ate a huge feast with more than a dozen devout Catholic Potawatomi who told all kinds of family stories as we sat around Marge's large round table. Marge is the oldest of these 4th generation descendants of little Teresa. I sat near her three brothers, Jim, Bob and Jerry, each of who told me stories punctuated with lots of laughter. And there was Virginia Pearl, the energetic nun of the sisters of St. Joseph who is the sort of nun that would inspire any little girl to consider the "religious vocation" a wonderful option for her life.

Virginia (just call me "Ginger") Pearl never intended to be a nun and even tried to avoid it in college by plentiful dating. But she expected at least one in the family would enter a religious vocation. She expected it to be Bob, but he joined the Army (though later on became a Eucharistic Minister). Then she hoped the order would reject her but now she says, "once I crossed the threshold of the convent I never again had any doubts." "Ginger" is a chaplain at a state hospital and lives on (and works on) an ecumenical organic farm with several from other orders and two Mennonite families. I don't know how old she actually is—she might be 65 or she could be 75, but she acts about 35. She is the sort of Potawatomi who could have walked this trail and lived. *She still might!*

I spent the entire afternoon and evening with the laughing-loving Pearl family. We ate together, looked at photos together, told stories together, and prayed together. They are a forgiving family and, while condemning the injustice, they (like Peggy and others) showed no bitterness. Ginger explained how her mother had told of the horrors of the past, yet always with the closing admonition, "But we must not get bitter."

At first I felt like a stowaway at a family reunion but before long I was included as if I was one of these big strapping brothers and energetic retirement-aged women who were still active. We sat around the table until it was almost dark and I needed to head back to Kansas City to the airport. After a thousand pictures or so I was escorted out the door and bid farewell with plentiful hugs.

I drove to the airport in the gathering darkness full of grace… grace that was mediated by Peggy Kinder's family and the Pearl family of Potawatomi Indians. Nothing any of us can do will take away the wrongness of the Indian removals and the repeated breaking of treaties by our government. But these two families brought healing and reconciliation to me personally. After walking in the steps of their forebears for two months I got to actually meet and love—but more, *to be loved*—by the descendants of the survivors.

What happened in 1838 was wrong—it was a national sin. Like all sin the remedy is *spiritual*—confession, repentance, penance, restitution and reconciliation.

Peggy Kinder -- three generations of descendants of Daniel Bourassa

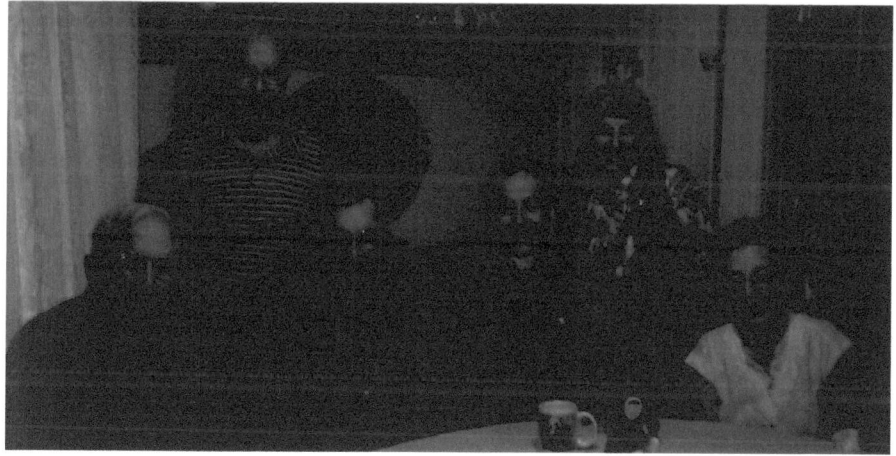

Three brothers and two sisters of the Pearl family
Sister Virginia "Ginger" Pearl standing at back on right

THE REST OF THE STORY...
What happened after the Trail of Death ended?

Dr. George Jeroloman.
The oft-absent doctor for the emigrating party was only 27 years old when he accompanied the emigration. He had graduated from Union College in Schenectady, New York and rowed himself from Ft. Wayne to Logansport but his rowboat capsized and he lost all his medicines. He thus relied on natural medicines for sicknesses and there was always "bleeding" a patient, which was so popular at the time. He was sick for much of the Trail of Death journey, staying in nearby towns. The Indians tried to get him expelled from the party but Polke suggested they were free to not use his services but he would be retained for the officers. On returning from the trek he increasingly practiced farming more than medicine and after a successful and lucrative career in farming built a large house at the corner of Walnut and 10th street in Logansport which is the present day home of the Cass County Historical society. He lived until March 4, 1883, dying at the age of 72 and was generously praised by his hometown newspaper. He was not remembered well for his role on the Trail of Death.

General Tipton
Indian-hater Tipton left the party just after Danville, Illinois and returned to Logansport with 85 or so of the Indiana volunteer militia since his authority expired at the Indiana state line. He continued to send and receive letters from those on the journey as if he were still in charge in some way, though it is not clear he was officially in charge. Maybe his position as the former Indian agent and (perhaps more so) as a U.S. Senator and his ties with the Governor of Indiana gave him this sort of standing with Polke and even Father Petit who also wrote to him regarding promised money for the new mission and education for the Indians. But he did not influence things long. After return to Logansport, his young wife died within five months. Then on March 3 his term in the U.S. Senate ended and just a month afterward, on April 5, 1839 Tipton himself died in his home at Logansport, just seven months after he commanded the round up of the Potawatomi at Twin Lakes. Some say the Indians pronounced a curse on him. Whatever, the man is oft cursed today by both white and red men for his heavy-handed role in this ugly affair.

Judge William Polke
Judge Polke did not leave for home right away. He may have left his son with the Potawatomi as he promised, then returned to Independence to wrap up the organizational and financial details of the journey. While he was

waiting on the arrival of agent Davis he visited friends—actually relatives—who lived nearby: his brother-in-law McCoy with whom he had taught at the Indian school in Niles, Michigan, and his brother Robert Polke who was an Indian trader. Polke kept a "continuation journal" during this time so we have access to some data on his delayed departure. In the mean time his horses were stolen which was a considerable financial loss since a good horse could cost more than $50. Agent Davis finally showed up on December 1, almost a month after the Potawatomi arrived. Polke certinly communicated to Davis the promises made. Polke left the area December 4 and headed for Independence where he planned to catch a stagecoach to St. Louis where he probably intended to travel by steamboat down the Mississippi, then up the Ohio and Wabash to Logansport. Did he make it by Christmas? Perhaps—but it would have been a stretch and every connection would have to work perfectly. More likely Mrs. Polke celebrated Christmas alone on this year. A few years after returning to Logansport, Polke was appointed Registrar of the land office in Ft. Wayne and moved there. He died in 1843, five years after leading the Potawatomi to Kansas. He was 68 years old. His grave has never been found.

Chief Menominee
Menominee, "the Potawatomi preacher," had refused to sign the treaties selling his land and was confined with several other chiefs to a jail wagon until Father Petit arrived in Danville, Illinois, and got him released (just as General Tipton left, probably no coincidence). Having not signed away his land, the government leaders simply refused to consider him a "Chief" but only as one of the "head men" even though he was a signatory on four major treaties before the dastardly 1836 treaty which he had refused to sign. He probably was about 48 years old when he was forcibly removed to Kansas without receiving any payments for his land. Did he survive the journey? He did. He was among the Potawatomi who relocated from the Government's drop-off point to Sugar Creek and he lived another three years. He died at the St. Mary's Mission on Sugar Creek April 15, 1841, and according to the Jesuit record was buried there. He was about 50 year old. The statue at the start of this journey was erected long after and was erected by the state of Indiana remembering his stance of character and is somewhat of a confession of the state's sin.

Father Petit
Petit, the priest to the Potawatomi, had been commanded by his Bishop to stay long enough to hand over his congregation to the Jesuit priest assigned to them in Kansas. He did this but waited for his next orders from his Bishop back in Vincennes, Indiana. Soon he took sick with the fever again (as he had often on the journey). This time he was cared for in the home of Baptist

Indian Joseph Bourassa for almost three weeks, probably not right in the camp but somewhere nearby. When he did recover (19 days later) he returned again to the camp in late November while still awaiting a letter from his Bishop. He describes the Potawatomi camp in his daily diary as, *"I return to camp—a church has been built there of bark and pieces of wood set upright, they are building an Indian lodge for us.* Just a few days before Christmas 1838 he received his Bishop's letter instructing him to return. He arranged his gear for the return journey—both by selling unneeded things and buying some others. He bought a bearskin for his saddle for $2.25, perhaps to minimize the pain of his saddle sores. He also bought a new bridle, some hay and a pair of moccasins and overshoes. He paid back $6 he had borrowed from Joseph Morlin and sold his ax and old bridle. He records five people paying back loans he had made to both whites and Indians. But there is one line of receipts that is packed with meaning—it simply says, *"Present from the Indians on my departure--$21.00"* Here we catch a glimpse of the tender love his congregation had for him. The poor Indians barely surviving on their own collected $21 for their beloved priest—a gift from the poor to the poor. I wish I could have seen the emotion present at that occasion. Still weakened by the fever and thumb-sized sores over his body, Petit left for Indiana the day after New Year's day, January 2, 1839, accompanied by his faithful Potawatomi assistant, Abram Burnett.

<u>Father Petit arrived in St. Louis 13 days later, on January 15</u>, intending to take a steamboat home once the Wabash River thawed in spring. He arrived in St. Louis exhausted and once more came down with "the fever." Until now he had only described the agony of the Potawatomi in the trek but on January 18, 1839 he wrote to his Bishop describing his own anguish. *"After a horseback ride of 160 miles I found it impossible to continue: my weakness growing worse every day... The good Lord permitted me to make this journey with an open sore on the seat, another on the thigh, and a third on the leg— the remainder of the numerous sores which covered my whole body during my illness at the Osage River."* Here he was under the care of the Jesuits at what is now St. Louis University. He closed his hopeful letter to his superior with *"I close, thinking that I shall be restored in a fortnight, and that, when the Wabash opens, I shall have the long-denied happiness of receiving your benediction."*

<u>Petit did not leave in a fortnight</u>. He weakened and on February 10 he died in the hand of the Jesuits who were caring for him. He was 28 years old.

Father Petit was buried then in St. Louis until 1856 when his body was brought back to St. Mary's Lake, now the site of the University of Notre Dame where it now lies under the floor of his replica log chapel.

The Mission Band of the Potawatomi

As mentioned earlier, the Potawatomi did not stay at the drop-off site near Osawatomie, Kansas, but relocated 20 miles south to the new St. Mary's Mission where they came under the spiritual direction of Father Hoecken and Mother Rose Philippine Duchesne, a Catholic sister who gave herself to tangible acts of service and to prayer. But the Sugar Creek location was not to last. As always the US Government got a new idea. In 1848 the government decided all the Potawatomi west of the Mississippi should be gathered in one place, so the generation that had endured the removal from Indiana, now were removed another 150 miles west to St. Mary's on the Kansas river where the Catholics once again opened another school for them. They remained here another 20 years until the Civil War when, threatened by both the Confederate forces and the Plains Indians, the railroad bought their land in Kansas so they moved to Oklahoma signing yet another treaty. Today many Potawatomi can be found in Kansas and Oklahoma though they are also found in Indiana, Wisconsin, Michigan, Canada and throughout the USA. They are spiritually devout people and many still are highly devoted Roman Catholics and Baptists.

For further reading

1. Willard, Shirley and Susan Campbell, *Potawatomi Trail of Death: 1838 Removal from Indiana to Kansas.* Rochester, Indiana: Fulton County Historical Society, 2003.
>This should be the first book you get if you are intrigued and want to read more about the Trail of Death. In this large book Shirley and Susan have collected in one place some of the other works that are now out of print, including Irving McKee's book below, the entire journal of the emigrating party, reproductions of George Winter's art, and a dozen other articles and reprints on the Potawatomi and the Trail of Death. This book is available from the Fulton County Historical Society in Rochester Indiana (37 E 375 N, Rochester, Indiana 46975). If you are from Indiana just stop by the "round barn on US 31" the next time you pass near Rochester, Indiana and pick one up or go to http://www.potawatomi-tda.org/

2. McMullen, John William, *The Last Black robe of Indiana and the Potawatomi Trail of Death.* Casper, Wyoming: Charles River press, 2006
>If you like historical novels consider this novel based on the life of Benjamin Petit that was being written simultaneously with my walk on the trail. McMullen is a third order Benedictine Oblate and high school teacher in Evansville, Indiana. His book became available just after I finished editing this manuscript. Once one is familiar with the primary sources of this story, it is fun to read one writer's understanding of what might have happened. For me it fed my continuing interest in this dedicated shepherd of his flock—Father petit. ISBN 0-9791304-0-9

3. Other major resources available in some libraries:

Armstrong Robertsson, Nellie and Dorothy Riker, editors. *The John Tipton Papers, Volume III, 1834-1839. Indiana Historical Collections, Volumne XXVI.* Indianapolis, Indiana: The Indiana Historical Bureau, 1942

McKee, Irving. The Trail of Death; Letters of Benjamin Marie Petit. Indianapolis, Indiana: Historical Society press, 1941

Polke, William. "The Continuation of the Journal of an Emigrating Party of Potawatomi Indians, 1838 and Ten William Polke Manuscripts." *Indiana Magazine of History*, 44 (1948): 393-408

"We have now arrived at our journey's end. The government must now be satisfied. We have been taken from homes affording us plenty, and brought to a desert - a wilderness - and are now to be scattered and left as the husbandman scatters his seed."

– ***Pe-Pish-kay's speech***
Monday 5th November
Osawatomie, Kansas
[from the official journal]